Otherness and Power
Michael Jackson
and His Media Critics

Susan Woodward

ISBN: 978-0-578-13802-2 (sc)
ISBN: 978-0-578-13817-6 (e)

Blackmore Books rev. date: 5/1/2014

BLACKMORE
BOOKS

CONTENTS

CHAPTER ONE

INTRODUCTION

Michael Jackson's adult career spanned approximately thirty years, during which time he accrued many millions of ardent fans. His fans saw him as a phenomenally talented singer, songwriter, dancer and producer whose personality seemed to have a sweetness not seen in other pop musicians and a mercurial quality that made him more fascinating to many than other performers of his era.

People who worked with Jackson reported him to be shy, gentlemanly and often genuinely childlike. He was not known to throw his weight around with other musicians, throw entitled tantrums, abuse employees or assault the paparazzi who relentlessly plagued him. People who knew him have remarked on his empathy for others and his extraordinary kindness.

The media, especially in the U.S. and Britain, frequently painted a completely different picture of Jackson. Although he had been seen as eccentric since the early days of his adult fame, the ridicule and vitriol began in earnest in 1984, during the planning of a concert tour with his brothers, and only grew over time. As details of the tour, called the Victory tour, emerged, Jackson was suspected of exploiting his fans' adulation in the interest of his commercial success. But after the tour was long behind him, Jackson continued to be mocked, sometimes in hateful language, for perceived eccentricities and his changing appearance, and his remarkable talent was often treated dismissively. When he was twice accused of sexually abusing children, most journalists seemed certain of his guilt and did not consider the possibility that Jackson might innocent. A large segment of the public assumed that they were being given an accurate portrayal by reporters and came to adopt as received wisdom the media's negative representation of Jackson.

How did two such dramatically opposing views of one individual come about? How could Jackson's fans and many in the media, who after all were reacting to the same set of information, come to such different conclusions, each side fully believing that they were right?

Two reasons have typically been given by Jackson fans for the negative media responses to Jackson: racism and deep discomfort with his "otherness," meaning his supposed eccentricities and his fluid identity signifiers. While these reasons have seemed to me to be obviously true, I had the persistent feeling that there was something else going on. After studying hostile writings about Jackson I began to see that there was another factor to which journalists were reacting, with distrust or even fear: a perception of extraordinary power.

Jackson is often said to have been as famous as the Beatles or Elvis Presley. The Beatles and Elvis were criticized and even to some degree feared by the older generation due to their influence over young people. The negative reaction to Jackson was not generational; his detractors were as likely to be progressive, young (mostly white) people, as well as older people. Jackson's critics were responding to a radically different quality than that possessed by Elvis or the Beatles:

that of a royal or elite person or of even a supernatural being. And this extraordinary power originated from Jackson's otherness.

The perception of Jackson as "other" sprang from his fluid and unreadable identity as well as some of his behavior. The fluid, unreadable traits were his race (he was African American, although, to greatly complicate matters, he appeared to become white), gender (he was clearly male, but a man who was very comfortable with feminine attributes such as a high singing voice, soft speaking voice, an interest in fashion and make-up), sexuality (speculation abounded that he was gay or that he was a pedophile or that he was just asexual), and age (as a child he seemed to be very adult, but as an adult he was notably childlike). His otherness also came from his sometimes unconventional behavior and lifestyle (Neverland, making public appearances with his chimpanzee, and not living with his second wife are examples) and even from the level of his talent as a singer and dancer.

Jackson's otherness has perhaps has been most eloquently described by Susan Fast in her article "The Difference That Exceeded Understanding: Remembering Michael Jackson": "These differences were impenetrable, uncontainable, and they created enormous anxiety. Please be black, Michael, or white, or gay or straight, father or mother, father to children, not a child yourself, so we at least know how to direct our liberal (in)tolerance. And try not to confuse *all* the codes simultaneously."[1]

I have selected for this book three examples of writing in which the perception of Jackson's power, and discomfort with it, is made explicit. Unlike the works I have chosen to examine, much of the criticism in the media came in the

---

[1]   Susan Fast, "The Difference That Exceeded Understanding: Remembering Michael Jackson (1959-2009)," *Popular Music and Society*, Vol. 33, No. 2, May 2010.

form of tabloid stories or dismissive reviews of albums or performances. (For a good example, see Jon Pareles, "Michael Jackson Is Angry, Understand?", *New York Times*, June 18, 1995.) By contrast, the works I have selected are lengthy, detailed pieces that critique Jackson's life and career in a comprehensive way, rather than focusing on one work or one performance. I believe, however, that the tabloid stories and dismissive reviews also are reacting to Jackson's unusual power, although they do not usually state it explicitly, as do the authors whose works I analyze here.

All of the authors analyzed in this book perceive Jackson as "other," although in somewhat different ways, and they perceive him as powerful in different ways. In every case, however, the power they feel that Jackson had derived from not just his fame and wealth but also from his otherness.

The first work I consider is *Trapped: Michael Jackson and the Crossover Dream*, a book by music critic Dave Marsh, published in 1985, at the height of Jackson's fame. I also examine an article by journalist Maureen Orth, published in *Vanity Fair* magazine in 2003, apparently in response to the airing of the documentary *Living with Michael Jackson*. The last work is *The Resistible Demise of Michael Jackson*, edited by Mark Fisher, and published in 2009, a few months after Jackson died. This book is a collection of essays by 23 music writers, bloggers and academics, most of them British.

These writers' discomfort with and even anger at Jackson's otherness are not disguised, but the same could not be said for racist feelings. While I believe that some degree of racism may be present in these three works, it is not made explicit, with a few exceptions, therefore it is difficult to address directly. Of course, being African American was an element of Jackson's otherness, so racist feelings were often part of the discomfort that some felt with his otherness.

The primary purpose of this book is not to mount a point-by-point response to all of the baseless assumptions and incorrect facts contained in these pieces, but doing some of that is unavoidable. Unless otherwise noted, I will only use the knowledge of Jackson that was available to the writers at the time of publication of their works.

The media's most damaging assumption about Jackson was that he was a child molester. Based on what I have read of the circumstances and details of the allegations of child sexual abuse and of Jackson's character, I do not believe that Jackson molested children or had a sexual interest in children, despite the more recent allegations by Wade Robson. I am not going to address the child abuse issue in great detail since doing so would turn this into another sort of book entirely. The child abuse issue has been explored quite thoroughly and competently elsewhere, most notably in "Was Michael Jackson Framed?" by Mary A. Fischer, *GQ*, October 1994; *Michael Jackson Conspiracy* by Aphrodite Jones (2007); and *My Friend Michael: An Ordinary Friendship with an Extraordinary Man* by Frank Cascio (2011). In any case, the hostility of the media towards Jackson began years before the first accusations of child abuse, and later antagonism from the media was not necessarily solely in response to those allegations, as we will see.

As someone who has read exhaustively about Michael Jackson and has very positive feeling about him, in the course of doing research it was difficult to read so many works that are harshly critical of him. I understand that many who read this book may have the same difficulty with the content of the works I analyze and may wonder what value there could be in repeating damaging or false stories. My goal, however, is to understand more about Jackson's cultural impact by understanding more about his critics, as well as to examine how we treat those who are seen as different or "other." And out of that negativity of these critics comes a surprisingly positive view of Jackson's power as an artist.

5

CHAPTER TWO

AMERICAN MESSIAH

M ichael Jackson's album *Thriller* was released on December 1, 1982. It quickly became the best-selling album of all time, and it remains so today. In May 1983, Jackson performed "Billie Jean" on Motown's 25th anniversary TV special, electrifying viewers with his dancing and further spurring interest in *Thriller*. In December 1983, Jackson's music video of "Billie Jean" debuted on MTV after his battle to get the channel to air its first video by a black artist. In May 1984, Jackson was invited to the Reagan White House to meet the President and accept an award for helping to promote a campaign against teen drunk driving. But possibly his greatest accomplishment was that of bringing down racial barriers in a segregated music scene and revitalizing a declining music industry through the massive success of *Thriller*.

Jackson, of course, had been since childhood the star of the Jackson 5, but by the time of the release of *Thriller* he no longer was interested in performing with his brothers. However, he reluctantly agreed to join them for a last series of concerts, the Victory tour, after being pressured by his family. The announcement of the tour, in September 1983, was greeted with tremendous excitement, because Jackson had not performed live since *Thriller*'s release. But as problems emerged with the tour's planning, the mood of the media and the public changed. The public was dismayed at the $30 ticket price, which was very high for that time, and the requirement that tickets be bought in blocks of four, a scheme that many felt would exclude underprivileged fans. Jackson and his brothers were further criticized for not playing in areas where many of their African American fans lived. Out of this debacle came the first really scathing criticism of Jackson by the media. Jackson sought to undo some of the damage by enabling fans to buy single tickets, giving away tickets to fans who could not afford the $30 price and declaring that he would give all of his profits to charity. However, his announcement did not put an end to the media's criticisms.

Among the journalists who found fault with Jackson at this time was Dave Marsh, a music critic who had written a bestselling book about Bruce Springsteen. In December 1985, Marsh published *Trapped: Michael Jackson and the Crossover Dream*, the first book-length criticism of Jackson. The structure of the book is unusual. *Trapped* consists of chapters in the form of open letters addressed to Jackson, alternating with chapters of detailed, well-researched biography. While the biography chapters are even-handed in tone, the open letter chapters are harshly critical. The tenor of the alternating chapters is so strikingly different that it is as if *Trapped* is two books sandwiched together.

I will focus on the open letter chapters. Marsh says that he is writing these open letters because he assumes that Jackson would not talk to him. He says that "there was no way to compel a dialogue," so he relies upon interviews Jackson had given to other journalists and his own observations of Jackson's career.

Marsh began as a passionate fan who saw Jackson as someone with the power to bring an unprecedented unity to

American, or even world, society, or at least to represent the dream of that unity.

> You soared higher than any other pop star has
> ever climbed. . . . In those months of your rise,
> the very name Michael Jackson became a totem.
> The bond between you and your fans seemed so
> powerful that it would overwhelm all barriers,
> cross over all boundaries. That bond was a version
> of a dream, its expression essentially American
> but truly worldwide, in which all opposites
> are reconciled, sexual and racial and political
> contradictions extinguished or, rather, fused one
> unto the other, through sheer goodwill . . . .
> The dream of which I speak is too utopian to be
> realized, whether right here and now or in an
> afterlife. . . . But that makes it no less valuable as
> a dream, not as long as people cherish it. It's the
> one thing that might yet keep humanity from
> destroying itself, I think. . . .[2]

Marsh is specific about how Jackson's celebrity following the release of *Thriller* was able to offer that promise of unity.

> To me, your real victory with *Thriller* came when
> you united an audience of almost unprecedented
> diversity and forced blacks and whites, rich and
> poor, young and old, boys and girls, and all the
> rest, to recognize each other for an instant.[3]

Marsh, who is white and appears to be a man of liberal leanings, had placed his hope in Jackson as a figure who could finally ameliorate the terrible racial legacy of America.

---

[2] Marsh, *Trapped: Michael Jackson and the Crossover Dream* (1985), pp. 6, 7.
[3] Ibid., p. 205.

> But Michael Jackson is one thing before he is
> a singer or a success or a star or anything else.
> He is a black person in America. As a result, he
> set some chains to clanking, stirred some ancient
> ghosts, incited some venerable dreams. The ghosts
> of slavery and racism are four hundred years old
> but their power is fresh and strong. The dreams he
> incited are equally old – the fantastic hope that we
> can somehow be brought together long enough
> to lay those ghosts to rest. Give the dreams their
> names, too: Emancipation, integration, liberation.
> Or call them out with the term show business
> now uses: Crossover.[4]

Despite Marsh's perception of Jackson's great potential to heal social divisions, his feeling changed as a result of the machinations surrounding the Victory tour and the quality of the performances he saw. Marsh attended several of the tour's performances, including the opening and closing nights. He found all of the performances uninspired, mechanical and repeated exactly from night to night, and he felt that Jackson had a penchant to play to the cameras rather than the audience. Marsh was left with a feeling of profound betrayal.

> When the bond that wed us to you and your
> sense of joy was fractured – given even so much
> as a hairline wound – it felt as though the whole
> structure had collapsed and dragged us down with
> it . . . . You went from Mr. Do-No-Wrong to a
> *villain*.[5]

The fatal hairline fracture was initiated for Marsh by his perception that Jackson had betrayed his fans by his misusing his power only for commercial ends, exploiting his fans who

---

4   Ibid., p. 257.
5   Ibid., p. 8. Emphasis in the original.

bought high-priced tickets and then saw uninspired shows. This sense of promise and then betrayal is distilled in Marsh's analysis of the meaning of Jackson's wearing one glove: "With this one hand, I stay pure, untouched by reality as you know it; with the other hand, I manipulate your dirty world."[6] The disillusionment brought on by the Victory tour destroyed Marsh's "fantastic hope that we can somehow be brought together" and led him to conclude that "the story of Michael Jackson has simply burned out."[7]

Marsh understands that Jackson was pressured into participating in the Victory tour, saying twice that he was "trapped" by his family, and he knows that Jackson was not responsible for the ticket sales scheme, but this is not enough to alleviate his enormous sense of betrayal.

Although Marsh's criticisms begin with the Victory tour, he proceeds to attack Jackson on many fronts, most having to do with Jackson's supposed dishonesty with his fans, lack of self-awareness, and his otherness. Marsh sees Jackson as too motivated by commercial interests, not aware of the power he possessed to heal racial and other divisions, not aware of musical history, not aware of playing into racial stereotypes, not intellectually aware (Jackson is "a deck that is a few cards short"[8]), not grappling with his own issues of control and sexuality, and not behaving in a socially conventional manner. Given the detailed historical accuracy of the book's biographical chapters, it is surprising that many of Marsh's criticisms are without firm factual backing and based on assumptions.

Marsh cites evidence that Jackson betrays his fans. He feels cheated when Jackson appears in a TV advertisement for a special issue of *People* magazine devoted to Jackson and

---

[6]   Ibid., p. 247.

[7]   Ibid., p. 257.

[8]   Ibid., p. 76.

then finds that the magazine features no interviews of Jackson himself. He cites a press conference, called to dispel tabloid rumors: Jackson's manager attends the conference without him, indicating to Marsh that Jackson is not sincerely invested in communicating with his audience.

Marsh detects dishonesty in some of Jackson's art as well. He calls Eddie Van Halen's guitar solo on "Beat It" as a "one-shot gimmick."[9] He declares that Jackson "doesn't seem very interested in the content of [his] songs,"[10] but is more interested in numbers of records sold and dollars earned. He even sees dishonesty in Jackson's earliest days at Motown, when he was just 10 years old, saying, "You came into the music business living out a batch of fables and lies."[11] Among the fables and lies cited by Marsh are that Jackson's performance in the Jackson 5 song "I Want You Back," recorded when Jackson was 11 years old, is emotionally honest and that Diana Ross discovered the group.

Marsh sees another betrayal of the utopian dream that Jackson had seemed to embody when he fails to enlist his fans in his struggle to get his music played on white radio stations and his videos played on MTV. ". . . I'm pissed off because the opportunity to do just one little thing – to show people the lie on which racism is based – was squandered, thrown away, pissed upon."[12]

He expounds at length upon his certainty that Jackson is not aware of his black musical roots, specifically blues, gospel, rhythm and blues, and even country and bluegrass. He unfavorably compares Jackson to white musicians Bruce Springsteen, Bob Dylan, the Rolling Stones, the Beatles and Bill Munroe, and black musicians Chuck Berry and

9   Ibid., p. 80.
10   Ibid., p. 80.
11   Ibid., p. 74.
12   Ibid., p. 206.

Little Richard, all of whom, he says, are keenly aware of the African American roots of their music. Marsh's assumption is based upon his reading of Jackson's music, not upon any knowledge of Jackson's actual understanding of his musical roots.

As a further example of Jackson's lack of historical knowledge, Marsh focuses extensively on a tree trunk that is backstage at the Apollo Theater in Harlem and is traditionally touched by performers for good luck before going on stage. Although Jackson had performed at the Apollo, Marsh states, without citing evidence, that Jackson does not know the history of that tree trunk and how it came to be a good luck symbol. Marsh expounds upon the history of the tree trunk and black and white American popular music, thereby showing that he himself is well-versed in American musical history.

Marsh says that Jackson has recently "stumbled upon" a videotape of Mahalia Jackson and that, as a result, he began using gospel phrasing for the first time during the Victory tour. In fact, Jackson used gospel phrasing at least as early as the Triumph Tour in 1981, three years before the start of the Victory tour.[13]

Similarly, he declares that Jackson does not know the history of the moonwalk. He states that Jackson doesn't seem very interested in the content of his own songs and that it is surprising that he would be interested anything, such as Mahalia Jackson's performances, that happened as long as 30 years ago. He claims, remarkably, that Jackson is not even aware that his own grandfather listened to country music. Marsh offers no evidence for these assumptions.

---

[13] *The Jacksons Live* (CD), 1981. Marsh later contradicts himself when he states on page 254 that Jackson had been using "gospel ruminations" for years.

Marsh then compares Jackson to performers in minstrel shows. He claims that Stephen Foster, whose sentimental songs were widely used by minstrels, was "to minstrelsy what you are to contemporary pop,"[14] because Jackson's songs are escapist and feature love free of sexuality. And he portrays Jackson as a modern-day black minstrel performer, because, he claims, the many white people who bought *Thriller* saw in Jackson the minstrel stereotype of a "lazy, pretentious, frivolous, improvident, irresponsible and immature" black man "who loved to entertain whites."[15] Marsh insults Jackson and white fans when he says, "Ugly as it is to say, your appeal is intimately linked with fulfillment of these stereotypes."[16] He then insults Jackson's black fans when he says, "At least you gave them something to dance to, so they still love you."[17]

Jackson's references in interviews to magic, escapism, and dreams ignites considerable contempt from Marsh: "That you are essentially superstitious, bound by a belief in magic and the power of the unknowable, is all but beyond question,"[18] and he calls Jackson an intellectual "sloth" for his beliefs. He is scornful of Jackson's statements about songs coming to him from dreams or from God, rather than from conscious and deliberate hard work. "Michael, you speak of your songs arriving in dreams as if by magic. That's a central tenet of your campaign to convince the world that you're a truly unique figure, genuinely larger than life."[19]

In one form or another, he states repeatedly that Jackson is not self-aware or is confused about himself, but Marsh mistakes his own confusion for Jackson's: "Nobody was going to make much progress in figuring you out until you got a lot

---

[14]   Marsh, *Trapped*, p. 204.
[15]   Ibid., p. 204.
[16]   Ibid., p. 204.
[17]   Ibid., p. 207.
[18]   Ibid., p. 119.
[19]   Ibid., p. 47.

closer to figuring yourself out. You can't solve a puzzle that hasn't found its own solution. . . . If you were less confused about things, it would show. People would be less confused about you — maybe not their feelings about you, but at least less mixed up about who they think you are."[20] Marsh's discomfort with Jackson's unreadability is clear, although again he takes his own uncertainty for Jackson's: "Trying to get a firm fix on your image is like trying to bottle smoke. It sort of makes me wonder if you can get your image to hold still when you gaze into a mirror."[21]

Marsh's confusion about Jackson is particularly evident in the area of sexuality and conforming to expected gender roles. Despite stating that he believed Jackson when he denied being gay, Marsh expounds for many pages upon the reasons that people doubt Jackson's heterosexuality and repeats old rumors about his sexuality, implying that the rumors might be true. "People think you're gay, in a word, because you're pretty. This can inspire many resentments . . . . One of the epithets pretty boys like you are attacked with is that they're faggots. . . . In other words, Michael, people think you must be gay because you conform to a long-standing stereotype of what gay men are like."[22]

But what seems to bother Marsh more is his perception that Jackson simply is not interested in sex or has a fear of sex. "So what you're doing, in essence, isn't just denying an interest in homosexuality; you're denying the need for *any* sexual expression. You'll admit, I hope, that if this is not abnormal for a twenty-six-year-old human being, it is certainly highly unusual."[23] This is a striking criticism. Jackson seems to have been the only famous male pop musician who did not have

---

[20]   Ibid., p. 180.

[21]   Ibid., p. 74.

[22]   Ibid., p. 111.

[23]   Ibid., p. 112.

sex with groupies. One can easily imagine those other pop stars being criticized for their sexual license and Jackson being praised for having self-control and being more respectful of women; but Jackson was criticized (and not only by Marsh) for his reticence, and the sexual excesses of other pop stars has been considered to be too normal to be remarked upon by music journalists.

Marsh is disturbed by Jackson's 1979 interview with journalist Stephen Demorest, both by its content and the way in which Jackson insisted that the interview be conducted. During this interview, Jackson had his sister Janet repeat Demorest's questions to him before he would answer. Marsh does not see this as the joke it probably was, but as "extremely odd"[24] and arrogant. During the interview, Jackson tells Demorest that when he has a family he will adopt rather than "procreate."[25] Jackson questions the need to conform to typical expectations of how he should lead his life: "Who says at a certain age you have to get married? Who says at eighteen you've got to leave the house? I didn't drive until I was twenty, and I still don't want to."[26] Marsh's sarcastic take on this is, "That was just another one of your tirades about why Michael Jackson, the most special guy in the world, should never be asked to do anything except his absolute heart's desire."[27]

Demorest asks Jackson if he thinks it is possible to appreciate "escapism" too much. Jackson says, "No, I don't. There's a reason why God made the sunset red or purple or green. It's beautiful to look at – it's a minute of joy. There's a reason why we see rainbows after a rain, or a forest where deer come out. That wonder, that's escapism – it touches your

---

[24]   Ibid., p. 112.
[25]   Ibid., p. 112.
[26]   Ibid., p. 113.
[27]   Ibid., p. 113.

heart and there's no danger in that . . . and you say, 'God, is this wonderful – I do appreciate it."[28] Marsh's response to that is, "Well, Michael, if all that touches the heart is safe, then what about Hitler's appeal to the heartstrings of the German people?"[29]

Marsh takes a dim view of Jackson's life-long involvement with the Jehovah's Witnesses, seeing this as evidence of lack of intellect. One might think that disparaging another's religion might be off limits, but Marsh does not hesitate: "It's their [Jehovah's Witnesses'] illogic that sucks you in because it gives you the room for such studiedly childish pronouncements as . . . 'Science is so silly sometimes.'"[30]

He derides Jackson's love of childhood, linking it to his religion:

> I'd say what you like about the Witness worldview is the same thing you find in children's literature and cartoons, both forms of 'escapism' for which you express unbounded enthusiasm. . . . It [the church] asks nothing of you as an adult. It lays out rigid rules and regulations, a complete story of how the universe has unfolded, and a blueprint for what happens next, with heroes and villains and a happy ending for those who really deserve it. In its grip, you become a perpetual child, not responsible for anything that occurs.[31]

He even insults Jackson's belief in God: ". . . This belief in God as the agent by which all things occur is not Christian but pagan or, more precisely, barbaric."[32] Marsh implies that Jackson's religious beliefs make him a "savage," and he

[28] Ibid., p. 121.
[29] Ibid., p. 121.
[30] Ibid., pp. 120-121.
[31] Ibid., p. 122.
[32] Ibid., p. 121.

quotes James George Frazer's *The Golden Bough* as defining a "savage" as someone who cannot make the distinction between natural occurrences and the supernatural.

Marsh compares Jackson to artist Red Grooms and complains that, unlike Grooms, Jackson has no sense of humor. He cites the song "Rock with You," from the *Off the Wall* album, as a sad example of Jackson's inability to let go and have fun:

> On a record like "Rock with You," what comes through those happy-days lyrics is an unbearable sadness. It's expressed in the way you don't sing "all night," but leave it to the chorus, in the pleading way you phrase the word "rock," as though you weren't asking for sex but for something even more intimate.[33]

Marsh does not seem to have read in the liner notes for *Off the Wall* that the chorus consisted solely of Jackson's voice, negating his point that Jackson was too inhibited to sing the words, "all night."

―――― ∞ ――――

Dave Marsh's initial response to Michael Jackson after *Thriller* was released was to idealize him as a figure with the power to unite racial, sexual and political opposites in American society and even across the world. The "crossover dream" of the book's subtitle seems to have referred to Marsh's as well as Jackson's dream. His terrible disappointment in Jackson began with the commercial manipulations around the Victory tour, despite Jackson not being responsible for the tour's planning, and was furthered by other perceptions that Jackson was more interested in self-promotion than in being a

―――――――――

[33] Ibid., p. 182.

catalyst for social change. Another way to put it is that Marsh felt that Jackson did not understand that he had the power to promote social change or, worse, that he understood his power but chose to use it only for commercial gain.

But did Jackson understand his situation in the same way that Marsh did? Did he see himself as being in a unique position to unite social divisions or at least to promote the dream of social unity? Did he cynically misuse his enormous success just to garner more fame and more wealth?

The video for the Jacksons' "Can You Feel It," made in 1980 and based on a concept by Jackson, shows Jackson and his brothers bringing peace, unity and magic to the world, strongly suggesting that Jackson could have been envisioning a messianic role for himself at the time that *Thriller* was released two years later. And we know from the work that Jackson did after *Thriller*, beginning with "We Are the World," that he cared deeply about promoting compassion and bettering social conditions, especially for children.

However, Jackson seems to have had no such messianic intentions when he made *Thriller*. His first adult solo album, *Off the Wall* (1979), was critically well received and sold quite well. But he wrote about his terrible disappointment when he subsequently was awarded a Grammy in 1980 only in the Best R&B (read: black) Vocal Performance category. "I felt ignored by my peers and it hurt. . . . I said to myself, 'Wait until next time' – they won't be able to ignore the next album. . . . That experience lit a fire in my soul. All I could think of was the next album and what I would do with it. I wanted it to be truly great."[34]

Those words were published two and a half years after Marsh published *Trapped*, but the chapters of biography that alternate with the chapters of critique in *Trapped* also describe Jackson's response to the 1980 Grammys. Marsh

---

[34]   Michael Jackson, *Moon Walk* (1988), p. 176.

19

quotes Jackson as telling *Billboard* that "I cried a lot. My family thought I was going crazy because I was weeping so much about it."[35] Marsh concludes that Jackson "felt snubbed by his peers."[36]

Jackson's goal in making *Thriller* was to overcome racism and garner respect by making a "truly great" album that no one could ignore, that could not be shunted off into the R&B category in a music scene that was then very racially segregated. That goal was realized when *Thriller* earned eight Grammy awards, was critically acclaimed and sold in unprecedented numbers to both white and black fans. While Marsh was not alone in seeing Jackson as a unifying figure, there is no evidence that Jackson had the ambition to be a great uniter or that he understood that he might have had that power. It appears that the actions that Marsh saw as a betrayal of a nearly messianic power were just Jackson having a career, promoting himself, as all artists must do, and seeking to overcome the racism that had caused him to be treated dismissively. For Jackson, commercial success was an important element of overcoming racial barriers.

The dream of equality that Marsh envisioned in Jackson's art and persona could never have risen to a utopian level without the element of commercial success. The dream was utopian in part because Jackson could reach such a huge audience. If he had been an obscure artist, he would have been greatly appreciated by a few, but never could have engendered a dream of nationwide and worldwide unity.

Did Jackson actually have the power to be a great uniter? Could Jackson have been the catalyst to create a society "in which all opposites are reconciled, sexual and racial and political contradictions extinguished or, rather, fused one unto the other, through sheer goodwill"? This does not seem

---

[35]   Marsh, *Trapped*, p. 178.
[36]   Ibid., p. 178.

likely. Even the very high-minded Bob Marley had a limited ability to effect real change. Marley tried through his music to unite warring political factions in Jamaica and to increase black pride and historical awareness. While he did succeed in putting Jamaican music on the world map and making Jamaicans more proud of their racial and cultural heritage, he had no lasting effect on Jamaican political violence or any other aspect of Jamaican society. While Marsh may have complained about Jackson's abandonment of his power, Jackson, even without seeming to have Bob Marley's grand ambitions, still helped bring down racial barriers in the music industry. Reverend Al Sharpton even credited Jackson's acceptance by a broad white audience with helping to pave the way for the success of Oprah Winfrey, Tiger Woods, and Barack Obama.[37]

Marsh did not appear to have feared or resented Jackson's power, as do the other authors examined in this book; he *wanted* Jackson to recognize and use his power, to appropriate ends. But having been disappointed in Jackson's refusal or inability to take up the role as a unifier, Marsh then turned against him, listing all of the ways that he sees Jackson as other in an attempt to deny him of any power whatsoever. Marsh portrayed Jackson as a childish, ignorant, confused, although talented, person whose power was an illusion.

So Marsh made clear what he did not like about Michael Jackson. But who would Jackson have had to be to satisfy Dave Marsh? If we reverse his criticisms, we get a picture of who Marsh possibly thought Jackson should have been: someone who had little interest in commercial success (but just happened to be very commercially successful anyway so that he could still inspire the utopian dream of unity), whose music showed that he was firmly grounded in black musical traditions, who was self-aware and aware of

---

[37] Rev. Al Sharpton, speech at Jackson's memorial service, July 7, 2009.

21

his role as a catalyst for social change, who was obviously sexual (especially heterosexual), who was intellectual and not religious, who had no problem with losing control and having fun. However, artists rarely are so conventional. While Marsh described some of Jackson's statements and behavior as "bizarre," he seemed not to have realized that artists, especially extraordinarily gifted ones, tend to be at least mildly eccentric and feel the need to resist conformity in order to remain creative.

Marsh is very critical of Jackson's childlike qualities, seeing them as signs of lack of intelligence or sophistication. He seems to have been ignorant of the connection that many artists feel they must maintain with childhood in order to create. Artists such as Pablo Picasso, Salvador Dali, Martha Graham, Igor Stravinsky, William Blake, and many others, maintained strong ties to their childhoods in order to nurture their creativity.

Marsh is not sympathetic to Jackson's lack of conformity and does not fully understand that the power of Jackson's persona and art, to which Marsh responded so strongly at first, came from the very qualities that he later found so disturbing, Jackson's otherness. These the characteristics, Jackson's childlike persona and fluid racial and sexual qualities, are what lent Jackson such broad appeal, made him intriguing and exciting, and enabled fans such as Marsh to project onto him the power to change the world. Marsh, churlishly, states as much when he writes, "One key to your fame is that you fit the model of the outcast well enough to make other 'freaks' identify and want to help you out,"[38] although he does not elaborate on that idea. Instead of acknowledging the source of Jackson's power, he portrays the elements of his otherness as grave defects in an attempt to deny him credibility and agency.

---

[38]   Marsh, *Trapped*, pp. 201-202.

Marsh failed to understand that some of the behavior he found troubling may have been intended as humorous or have had a purpose that was not immediately discernible. For example, Marsh found disturbing that Jackson insisted that his interview with Stephen Demorest take place with his sister Janet repeating all questions to him before he would answer. Writer J. Randy Taraborrelli attempted to interview Jackson, under the same conditions, in 1981. Taraborrelli found the situation unworkable, ended the interview early and decided not to publish an article about it. Jackson's father later apologized to Taraborrelli, explaining that his son had not wanted to do any interviews at that time. Taraborrelli understood this to mean that Jackson did not want to be asked about the marital conflict that his parents were experiencing. Taraborrelli says he felt "a grudging admiration for the way Michael had gotten what he wanted. . . no story."[39]

Why would Dave Marsh begin by revering Jackson only to turn on him once perceived imperfections appeared? One of the lenses through which this puzzle can be seen is a psychological one, specifically a phenomenon known as splitting. Splitting is an ego defense mechanism, seen more commonly in some personality types than in others, of seeing the world in polarized terms of idealization or devaluation, all good or all bad, all black or all white, with none of the grays in between. This binary view defends against the anxiety of having to deal with the confusion of nuances. Although some people are much more inclined to perceive everything in this polarized way, everyone splits on occasion, especially when very angry (most typically in the form of "you're all bad, I'm all good").

One characteristic of this phenomenon is that sometimes a split completely flips. Something or someone who was

---

[39] Randy Taraborrelli, *Michael Jackson: The Magic, The Madness, The Whole Story* (2009), pp. 216-221.

previously seen as all bad or all good can suddenly appear to be the opposite. This is the basis of many a romantic comedy: a woman finds a man to be extremely annoying and tries to avoid him, until she suddenly sees him in a different light and falls in love.

Marsh himself declared early in his book that he was splitting, without using that term, and that his binary view of Jackson had flipped: "When the bond that wed us to you and your sense of joy was fractured – given even so much as a hairline wound – it felt as though the whole structure had collapsed and dragged us down with it . . . . You went from Mr. Do-No-Wrong to a *villain*." His initial feeling for Jackson as a messianic figure was clearly an unrealistic idealization that was destined for disappointment. Once that disappointment hit, Marsh devalued Jackson, seeing him as untrustworthy, confused and bizarre.

If Marsh had not started with such a highly idealized vision of Jackson, his reaction to disappointment would not have gone to the extreme of almost completely devaluing him. A similar lack of nuance is evident in the other works to be examined in the coming chapters, and the splitting evident in *Trapped* takes on a much more florid form.

CHAPTER THREE

WEB OF FEAR

Journalist Maureen Orth wrote five lengthy articles about Michael Jackson for *Vanity Fair* magazine. The first two articles, published in January 1994 and September 1995, were about the 1993 allegations against Jackson for child sexual abuse. Although Jackson's attorneys and investigator were interviewed by Orth, she painted an extremely negative picture of him and seemed to assume that he was guilty of abuse. She would go on to write two more articles, in March 2004 and July 2005, in response to the second round of allegations of child molestation, again seeming to assume that he was guilty. Orth wrote immediately after Jackson's death that she had become interested in writing about him, because she had a son who was about the same age as Jackson's accuser.[40]

The third of the five articles Orth wrote about Jackson was entitled "Losing His Grip" and was published in *Vanity Fair* in April 2003. This article appeared two months after the broadcast of a documentary by British journalist Martin Bashir called, "Living with Michael Jackson" and seems to

---

[40]   Maureen Orth, "Michael Jackson is Gone, But the Sad Facts Remain," *Vanity Fair*, June 2009.

25

have been written in response to that film. Although Bashir had promised Jackson that the documentary would show him in a positive light and that he would have final approval before it aired, Jackson never saw it before the broadcast and Bashir took pains to present Jackson in a negative light. The documentary was a public relations disaster for Jackson, especially the scene that showed him holding hands with a boy and talking about offering his bed to him. (Jackson never says in the film that he slept in the same bed with the boy, although his words were widely interpreted that way.) Several months later, this same boy accused Jackson of sexually abusing him.

Unlike Dave Marsh, Orth gives no sign that she had any appreciation of Jackson's talent or that she was ever sympathetic to him, although she wrote after his death that she had loved his music.[41] Like Marsh, she perceives Jackson in terms of his power, as well as his otherness, but she fears his power and feels that he uses it to manipulate and harm others.

At first glance, "Losing His Grip" appears to be well sourced, but a closer look tells a different story. A list of Orth's informants conveys the flavor of the article and a sense of its reliability:

- Myung-Ho Lee, Jackson's former financial advisor who was suing him for nonpayment
- Kathleen Kelly, an investment banker who had worked for Jackson and was suing him for nonpayment
- Robert Silverman, Myung-Ho Lee's lawyer
- journalist Victor M. Gutierrez, who was successfully sued for slander by Jackson in 1995 and who in 1997 wrote a scurrilous book about him
- Lisbeth Barron, Bear Stearns senior managing director
- Burt Fields, Jackson's lawyer in 1993 (quoted from 1993)

---

[41]   Ibid.

- William Hodgman, head of Los Angeles district attorney's office sex crimes unit
- Tom Sneddon, Santa Barbara County district attorney
- "a member of the prosecution team" (twice)
- "one member of the prosecution team"
- "two prosecution sources"
- "sources close to the prosecution"
- "someone on the prosecution team"
- "another member of the prosecution team"
- "sources close to [Jordie] Chandler's side" [Chandler is the 13-year-old boy who accused Jackson of molesting him in 1993]
- "one of the lawyers in the civil sex abuse case"
- Rod Lurie, a former reporter
- NBC reporter Diane Dimond, who for many years has reported negatively about Jackson
- Fox journalist Roger Friedman
- an unnamed ex-publicist of Jackson's
- Harry Benson, a photographer who worked with Jackson
- gossip columnist Rona Barrett
- Pat Murphy, author of *Santa Ynez Valley Secrets*
- Santa Ynez Valley real-estate agent Joe Olla
- a "well-connected resident of the Santa Ynez Valley"
- "a Sony executive quoted by the New York *Daily News*"
- "a former Sony official"
- "a former Sony employee"
- Charles Koppelman, a "music publisher" whose connection to Jackson is not explained [42]

---

[42] Koppelman formed a business partnership with Jackson in June 2003, two months after Orth's article was published. It is not clear whether Koppelman knew Jackson at all before their business partnership.

- Dr. Tina Alster, a "nationally recognized" dermatologist who never met Jackson
- an unnamed plastic surgeon who appeared on NBC's *Dateline*
- "medical professionals"
- the unnamed director of Warsaw's Royal Gardens
- "a man very familiar with the pop star's world"
- "sources formerly close to Jackson"
- "a source formerly close to Jackson"
- "other former [Jackson] employees"
- Jackson "insiders"
- "one close observer"
- "one person"
- "others"
- "I am told"

She also relies upon an affidavit by a deputy sheriff in Santa Barbara county, "various court papers" and "one [unnamed] published report." Of her approximately 55 informants, about two-thirds are anonymous.

Throughout the article are implications that people who talk about Jackson in unflattering ways can expect to be sued by him, thus seeming to explain the large number of anonymous informants. Orth says, "Jackson doesn't let much go by. . . ," referring to a penchant to sue those who speak out about him. But, in fact, Jackson only sued twice for slander or libel. Both of those cases will be discussed later.

No one in Jackson's camp would speak to Orth for "Losing His Grip," which is understandable given the extreme negativity of the two articles she had written previously after his defense team spoke to her at length. It appears that no one who had Jackson's best interests in mind and had good things to say would agree to be a source, named or unnamed, for a journalist so hostile to Jackson.

In addition to the obviously questionable quality of her sources, Orth states a number of assumptions and assertions without presenting reasonable alternate views or, apparently, fact-checking.

"Losing His Grip" is a catalogue of the ways in which Jackson's behavior is unacceptable and the ways in which Jackson is other, not like "us." Orth begins with a description of two voodoo rites that Myung-Ho Lee told her were performed, at huge expense, for Jackson and a third rite that Lee said he refused to help Jackson arrange. One of the rites was said to have been performed by a "voodoo chief" in Mali, whose ceremony entailed the ritual slaughter of 42 cows. The other rite, conducted by a "voodoo doctor and a mysterious Egyptian woman named Samia," required Jackson to bathe in sheep's blood. The ceremony that Lee said he refused to help arrange involved the slaughter of numerous birds and small animals.

This is, in its way, the perfect scene with which to begin her article, incorporating white racial fear, violence and useless expenditures of hundreds of thousands of dollars, themes that run throughout the article. As though concerned that Myung-Ho Lee's name alone might throw him into the "other" category with Jackson, Orth notes that he is "U.S.-educated." In addition to the obvious fact that Lee's lawsuit would render him a questionable source, the story of the voodoo rites is contradictory to everything known about Jackson, who loved animals, was a vegetarian for many years and had a decades long grounding in a Christian church.

The actual inspiration for Lee's story of the voodoo ceremonies may be something that Jackson himself said to journalist J. Randy Taraborrelli in 1995, in expressing his enormous frustration with the media's fabricated or wildly inaccurate stories about him: "Why not just tell people I'm an alien from Mars. Tell them I eat live chickens and that I do a voodoo dance at midnight. They'll believe anything you say, because you're a *reporter*. But if I, Michael Jackson, were to say, 'I'm an alien from Mars and eat live chickens and do a voodoo dance every night at midnight,' people would say, 'Oh, man, that Michael Jackson is *nuts*. He's cracked up. You can't believe a word that comes out of his mouth.'"[43]

The theme of white racial fear is touched on again when Orth refers to Jackson's "apparently white" children. She later claims that Jackson said in the Bashir documentary that he wants to "obtain" (rather than "have" or "adopt") more children, although he never used that word. If he had been a white celebrity who had children of color, it is unlikely that the apparent racial difference between him and his children would be remarked upon except in a positive way.

Orth describes observing Jackson in a courtroom in Santa Maria, California in early December 2002. Orth describes his appearance as "amazing," saying that he wore a wig and white make-up, and she repeats the false story that he had a prosthesis to replace the tip of his nose. She did not say that she actually saw the prosthesis, but assumes that it was concealed by make-up. She is critical of his repeated testimony that he cannot recall things that she believes he actually can recall and his many requests to have attorneys repeat questions. Orth reports that Jackson makes "mischievous gestures" from the witness stand, which his lawyers say was in response to being baited by spectators. She remarks that she did not see the baiting, implying that it never happened.

Jackson was in court because he was being sued by concert promoter Marcel Avram for pulling out of two concerts. Orth does not mention the fact that six months before those two concerts were to take place Jackson seriously injured his back during a performance in Munich when a stage prop on which he was standing fell approximately 30 feet.

---

[43] Taraborrelli, *Michael Jackson: The Magic & The Madness* (2009), p. 578. Emphasis in the original.

Orth says, without citing a source, that the week before she observed Jackson in court he had made another court appearance during which he "was monosyllabic, dazed, and disheveled, and the tip of his nose seemed to be missing, owing to exaggerated amounts of plastic surgery." She seems to be referring to the court appearance he made in which he was unshaven and had a strip of tape on the bridge of his nose, a detail that caused a flurry of media speculation about the state of his face and the amount of plastic surgery he may have had.

The rumor, which had been circulating for many years, that the tip of Jackson's nose was missing and that he had to wear a prosthesis was conclusively disproven in 1998, although the media took little notice. Jackson had sued the *Daily Mirror*, a British tabloid, for an article it published in 1992 claiming that the tip of his nose was missing and that his face was hideously disfigured and scarred by plastic surgery. The lawsuit was settled, by an apology from the *Daily Mirror*, in November 1998 after doctors and representatives from the *Mirror* examined Jackson's unmade-up face for 40 minutes.[44] The persistence of this rumor and the scarce notice given to its refutation is a good example of the damage that can be done by false media stories.[45]

Orth goes on to assert that Jackson's philanthropy is a myth, that his charitable giving does not materialize and that his charitable organizations do nothing. The lack of charitable donations that she notes and the problems with his charitable foundations, if true, date from 1996. She does not

---

[44] See "Mirror cracks in apology in Jackson suit," *Variety*, November 10, 1998, and "Michael Jackson settles case," *The Independent*, November 10, 1998.

[45] For an excellent examination of the rumors of Jackson's plastic surgery, see Willa Stillwater's brilliant book *M Poetica* (2011). Dr. Stillwater uses logic and a review of photographs to show that the media's claims about his plastic surgery were greatly exaggerated.

mention that since 1996 he continued involvement in charity through personal appearances and donations of costumes and memorabilia to be auctioned, even if he did not always donate money.[46]

She says that Jackson was in Germany during the filming of the Bashir documentary to receive lifetime achievement and humanitarian awards, suggesting that the latter was a continuation of his pretense of being a philanthropist. However, as is made clear from the documentary, he was not in Germany to receive a humanitarian award. He was in Germany to receive a Bambi Award[47] for "Pop Artist of the Millenium," and while in Germany he donated a jacket to be auctioned for charity.

Orth talks to several residents of the Santa Ynez Valley, where Jackson's home, Neverland, is located. An unnamed "well-connected resident" of the Valley tells her that Jackson's employees rarely talk to outsiders because "they're all scared to death they'll be sued. He has a large legal team." But this same person tells Orth that Jackson's employees do in fact talk and that those "who have seen him in close contact say he's gotten stranger and stranger in the last two years." Without citing a source, Orth says that Jackson does not participate in the Valley's "lively party circuit," suggesting that Jackson's neighbors see him as an outsider.

Orth talks to Pat Murphy, the author of *Santa Ynez Valley Secrets*, a book apparently devoted to local gossip. Murphy says that area residents became "suspicious" of Jackson when he required employees to sign confidentiality agreements. "More and more stories came out about how reclusive Michael was.

---

[46] See Adrian Grant, *Michael Jackson: A Visual Documentary* (2009). This book is an exhaustive narrative of Jackson's activities told through the public record.

[47] A German media award for "the heroes of our time who have touched and inspired us with their actions, talents and visions," according to the Bambi Awards website.

Then people started pulling away, because he was so strange." Murphy does not elaborate on what she means by "strange," but she states that "when Michael Jackson first moved to the valley he was a very nice-looking African-American man with brown skin. Now he's a white woman." This claim about Jackson's skin color is easy to fact-check. Jackson moved to the Santa Ynez Valley in May 1988, when his skin was already very light. Murphy's remark about Jackson becoming a "white woman" betrays her unease, and probably Orth's, with Jackson's ambiguous racial and gender signals.

Not long after Orth's article was published, Thomas Mesereau, Jackson's defense attorney for his 2005 trial for child molestation, visited Santa Maria, the town in the Santa Ynez Valley in which the trial would be held. He wanted to get a sense of how the locals, who would comprise the jury, felt about Jackson. After spending time in the community, he learned that people found Jackson to be "a nice person" and "a very decent and honest guy."[48] If Orth talked to anyone in that community who felt differently from the sources she used, she did not include them in her article.

Orth includes a summary of her two earlier articles about the sex abuse allegations brought against Jackson by Jordie Chandler in 1993. As in those articles, she does not present any facts in his defense. She adds a major new source, possibly her most blatantly unreliable named source, Victor M. Gutierrez, a journalist who wrote *Michael Jackson Was My Lover: The Secret Diary of Jordie Chandler*, which was published privately in 1997. In the unlikely event that Chandler kept a secret diary of his relationship with Jackson, it seems even more unlikely that he would have handed it over to a journalist. She describes details from Gutierrez's book as if they are the truth and says that her unnamed "prosecution sources" tell her that they believe the book to be accurate. Jackson successfully

---

[48] Aphrodite Jones, *Michael Jackson Conspiracy* (2007), p. 18.

sued Gutierrez for slander in 1995 after he claimed to have seen a videotape of Jackson having sex with a minor, but was never able to produce the tape.[49] This lawsuit was the second of the two times that Jackson ever sued for slander or libel.

An anonymous source tells Orth that Jordie Chandler (the boy who in 1993 accused Jackson of molesting him) and his family feared for their safety, and unnamed "member of the prosecution team" tells her that Chandler decided not to pursue criminal charges against Jackson because his safety and that of his family could not be guaranteed. These questionable sources do not offer any insight into who was threatening the Chandler family or any reasons to think that Jackson could have been involved, but the insinuation is clear.

Orth says that an unnamed prosecutor told her that Jackson purchased the silence of at least one boy who could have been a witness against him, adding, "Michael Jackson's sort of wealth buys an awful lot of favors." Orth concludes, based on anonymous informants in a prosecutor's office, that "so many witnesses they interviewed refused to come forward and were handsomely rewarded, while others who were willing initially to testify later reported being intimidated, harassed, and threatened." Similarly, Gutierrez tells her that Jackson bought the silence of parents. One of the unnamed prosecutors claims that they recorded investigator Anthony Pellicano, who worked for Jackson's attorney, begging one of Jackson's maids not to go to the police with information.

While Orth states this information as fact, she seems to have been unaware of the implications of such statements from prosecutors. In 1993, California had, and still has, a law, Penal Code 136.1, against "Preventing or Dissuading Victim or Witness from Attending of Giving Testimony."[50] This law

[49] "Michael Jackson Wins $2.7 Million Suit Against Writer," *Chicago Tribune*, April 10, 1998.
[50] Callagan, ed., *Penal Code 1993: Abridged California Edition*, page 15.

forbids preventing or dissuading, by any method, a victim of a crime or a witness from testifying in a trial or cooperating with law enforcement or prosecutors. If prosecutors had been aware of Jackson or Pellicano being involved in dissuading potential victims or witnesses from cooperating with the police or prosecutors, they could have, and no doubt would have, charged them with crimes. Since this did not happen, it is reasonable to assume that prosecutors had no evidence of Jackson and his associates dissuading anyone from cooperating with law enforcement.

In criticizing Jackson for his appearance, Orth cites an affidavit, probably dating from 1993, by Deborah Linden, a Santa Barbara county deputy sheriff, in which Linden quotes a former maid of Jackson's says that she was not aware of Jackson having a skin disease and that he bleaches his skin because he does not like black people. However, Orth admits that this same affidavit also states that Jackson had been diagnosed with lupus and that this disease could cause lightening of the skin.

Orth quotes an unnamed "nationally recognized" dermatologist, who never met Jackson, as declaring that he has body dysmorphic disorder, a psychiatric disorder in which one is obsessed with imagined physical defects and may resort to plastic surgery or other means to correct them. Another "nationally recognized dermatologist," Dr. Tina Alster, tells Orth that Jackson has body dysmorphic disorder, although Dr. Alster also never met Jackson. Similarly, Orth says that an unnamed plastic surgeon, who also never met Jackson, appearing on NBC's *Dateline*, affirms that Jackson may have had up to 50 surgeries on his face. Orth restates her assertion that Jackson had to wear a prosthesis on his nose due to lack of cartilage and then says, apropos of nothing, "According to medical professionals, if too many blood vessels are cauterized in the face, and blood is prevented from flowing to the skin, the skin can turn black and eventually wither away or fall off." She does not link this statement in any way to Jackson's plastic surgery or any other medical issues he may have had, but her statement implies that this is what has happened to Jackson's face.

After Jackson's *Invincible* album was released, he launched a public protest against his record company, Sony, in the summer of 2002, claiming that Sony was racist in not wanting to promote the album adequately. Orth calls this protest "amazing," but she then lends credence to his claims of feeling undermined by stating that Andrew Lack, who was installed as Sony chairman shortly after Jackson's protest, had in his previous job as president of NBC approved the airing of a *Dateline NBC* show devoted to Jackson's "collapsing face and the downslide of his career."

In addition to portraying Jackson himself as aberrant, Orth consistently describes his friends and associates in ways that suggest that they lead suspect lives. She characterizes Debbie Rowe, Jackson's second wife, as "a biker babe," his videographer F. Marc Schaffler as a producer of gay porn, and his plastic surgeon as someone "known for doing *Playboy* Playmates' breasts." His friend and "handler," as she calls him, Frank Tyson she notes was born Frank Cascio, a detail that suggests evasion or even a criminal a.k.a.

In her effort to paint him as bizarre, Orth refers to people who have nothing to do with Jackson. Among her sources who never met Jackson is an unnamed director of Warsaw's Royal Gardens. She quotes this person as telling *The Guardian* that he was "ready to believe the account of Jackson's aide, that the child abuse allegations were the work of an American religious sect enacting revenge for his refusal to sign up." The clear suggestion, through this unnamed, third-hand source, is that Jackson himself might have believed this explanation of why he was accused of molestation in 1993.

Laced throughout Orth's article are references to Jackson's power, but not the nearly divine power that Dave Marsh had initially attributed to him. Orth primarily describes Jackson in terms of wealth and celebrity and seems convinced that he uses his power to control and intimidate others. But Orth also depicts him as having a different kind of power: that of an elite, almost royal, person. In describing the scene at the court date she attended, Orth says that Jackson arrived "with the solemnity that would ordinarily be associated with the Popemobile," attended by security guards and aides. His clothes "suggest a private-school boy or a young member of European royalty," and in the courthouse he would speak only to children, "as if he were Santa Claus or the Dalai Lama." She quotes "a man very familiar with the pop star's world" as saying that Jackson wants to be seen as Walt Disney, Mozart, Elvis Presley and Fred Astaire. She cites a report in *The Guardian* that Jackson was thinking of buying a castle in Poland, where, she adds snidely, "the new king would reside."

But Orth suggests that he may not have come by his elite status honestly. She says, "Then there are the strategic friendships Jackson has so carefully cultivated," friendships with Uri Geller, Marlon Brando, Liza Minelli, Elizabeth Taylor, Rabbi Shmuley Boteach, and David Gest. (She admits, however, that Jackson has known Gest since childhood.) She does not explain why the friendships are "strategic" and why they would have to be "so carefully cultivated," but her words cast doubt on the reciprocal nature of these friendships and on Jackson's worth as someone with whom these famous people would want to associate, had they not been manipulated. In Orth's one suggestion that Jackson had supernatural power, she says that Geller "taught Jackson the fine points of telekinesis."

She insinuates at length that Jackson used Anthony Pellicano to do some of his dirty work. Pellicano, who worked for Jackson's defense attorney, Bertram Fields, at the time of the 1993 allegations, worked on Jackson's case for approximately six months. In 2008, Pellicano was convicted of wire fraud, wire-tapping and conspiracy, charges completely unconnected to his work on behalf of Jackson, but Orth makes extensive use of his now sullied reputation to cast doubt upon Jackson's character. At the time Orth's article was published, Pellicano had not worked for Jackson for over nine years.

She says that in 1993 Pellicano begged one of Jackson's maids not to go to the police with information and that "other former employees" were threatened by Pellicano and "still cower when they speak of him." Dissuading witnesses is a crime in California, as noted above, and Pellicano was never charged with this crime. Orth suggests other unproven criminality by Pellicano on behalf of Jackson. Victor Gutierrez claims that Pellicano harassed and threatened him. Diane Dimond, a reporter for NBC's *Dateline* who specializes in negative stories about Jackson, tells Orth that her car was broken into on some unspecified date and "our defense documents" were taken, after which she was given bodyguards. (Note that "defense documents" are not likely to have been related to reporting about Jackson, since his defense team would not have given documents to someone who could be counted on to use them to hurt him. And why would Pellicano want to steal Jackson defense documents?) Orth details three more stories of people, none of them connected to Jackson in any way, who believe they may have been threatened by Pellicano. She offers no proof, beyond the innuendo of connecting Jackson's name to Pellicano's, that Jackson was ever involved in or knew of any of the incidents, if they in fact occurred, and it is notable that Pellicano was never later convicted of threatening anyone.

Orth's impression of Jackson when she observes him in the courtroom is that he has the power to control the judge and the jury. She says that the judge seems "starstruck" and notes that the jury is "mostly white, female," suggesting that for that reason they will decide in Jackson's favor. She later pointedly adds that "Jackson is the [Santa Ynez] valley's most famous resident and is well known to the members of every jury pool," again implying that his celebrity can sway outcomes in court. This contradicts her implication elsewhere in the article that Jackson is regarded as bizarre and an outsider in the Santa Ynez Valley. (Despite her perception of Jackson's influence over the judge and jury, Jackson later lost Avram's suit against him.)

But beyond his fame and wealth, in Orth's view, the greater source of Jackson's power to influence and control others is his otherness, his unusual appearance and behavior and his refusal to play by conventional rules: "Apparently Jackson believes that the normal rules of conduct do not apply to him — that his extraordinary fame and talent entitle him to behave as he pleases." This idea is restated by one of the anonymous sources, "a man very familiar with the pop star's world," who says, "The rules that apply to the common folk do not apply to me [referring to Jackson]. I can get away with whatever I want to because I am Michael Jackson." Similarly, Santa Barbara district attorney Tom Sneddon tells Orth, referring to Jackson's behavior, "Of course. It's deliberate. I think it's frustrating that people let him get away with it. He's playing the fool and he fools people, but he doesn't fool everybody." Orth says, "This bizarre behavior often works to his advantage. The crazier Jackson appears, the more he is indulged and excused and not judged as a middle-aged man with serious obligations and responsibilities."

Why would a major, respected magazine publish an article that is poorly sourced, despite its number of sources, that relies so heavily upon innuendo, and that contains obvious biases and inaccuracies? The most obvious answer is that negative press about Jackson sold well. But there is a deeper answer to this question.

It appears that Orth's article is an effort to convince the reader that Jackson was a self-indulgent person who used poor judgment in controlling his finances, was bizarre in his appearance and in his behavior, and that he sexually abused children and got away with it by buying off and intimidating witnesses. However, as we have seen, Orth also describes him in terms of great power: the power of his wealth and fame and his ability to manipulate and fool others with his crazy behavior. But what is the point of painting this damning portrait?

The article functions in a way similar to Dave Marsh's criticisms of Jackson in that she seeks to discredit him. But unlike Marsh, Orth sees Jackson as dangerously powerful. The reader can sense her outrage and fear. This is an interesting reaction, since there were others who did not perceive Jackson that way at all and people who knew him described him as unusually empathic and kind.

Jackson seems to have been a deeply unsettling presence for Orth. She doesn't just see Jackson as a weirdo; she writes about him as if he is a threat that needs to be contained or neutralized. Orth spends nearly a third of her article on the child sex abuse allegations, so that is obviously a major focus of her concern. But the remaining two thirds of the article she uses to detail other objectionable behavior, little of which can be seen as a threat to anyone other than Jackson himself.

Dave Marsh's criticism of Jackson arose from his initially positive feeling about him, and we will see in the next chapter that extremely positive views of Jackson are often married to equally hostile views. Orth seems to have only a hostile opinion of Jackson. However, her fear of his power seems to stem from the positive reaction to him that others have. His power to influence and manipulate others is rooted in the positive feeling that so many have for Jackson, such as the judge and jurors in a courtroom or financial advisor Kathleen

Kelly who tells Orth that she still "believes" in Jackson, despite her lawsuit against him for nonpayment.

As we have seen, much of what Orth includes in her article lacks a credible source or is material that reasonably could have been interpreted in a different way. This is similar to the nature of Dave Marsh's criticisms, being based largely on assumptions or inaccuracies. Inaccurate stories about Jackson abounded in the media since at least 1983, and Marsh's book and Orth's article are well within that lineage.

Such questionably substantiated accounts of a person's life can be categorized as rumor or gossip, even if they are published in a major national magazine such as *Vanity Fair*. The study of the function of rumors and gossip shows that these false and damaging stories are often used to bully and control individuals or groups that the larger group perceives to be a threat to societal norms or the existing power structure.[51] This is a reflexive rather than conscious reaction to those seen as unacceptable or "other."

With the purpose of rumors and gossip in mind, Orth's article makes sense, as do most of the other gossipy, negative stories about Jackson that appeared over his adult career. It is unlikely that Orth understood that the goal of her article was to control or destroy Jackson. It is a common, if unfortunate, human reaction to malign those who don't fit in or who are perceived to transgress the social order.

Both Orth and Dave Marsh appear to be reacting to Jackson's perceived social transgressions. Orth seems to be trying to "correct" Jackson, to try to make him into the "middle-aged man with serious obligations and responsibilities" that he should be. This is similar to Marsh's

---

[51] Christine C. Kieffer, Ph.D., "Rumors and Gossip As Forms of Bullying: Sticks and Stones?" *Psychoanalytic Inquiry*, Vol. 33, Issue 2, March 2013, and Cass R. Sunstein, *On Rumors: How Falsehoods Spread, Why We Believe Them, What Can Be Done* (2009).

apparent wish that Jackson be a predictable, easily readable person who he could understand without effort.

Similar to Marsh, Orth seeks to deprive Jackson of his power by unmasking his perceived deceptions and deficiencies. Her main goal in writing the article appears to be to make the public aware of his true nature so that no one can be fooled by him in the future.

Orth not only lays out her case that Jackson is "bizarre" and that his behavior is unacceptable, but she also includes many references to his power. And therein lies the problem, from Orth's perspective. Someone as unconventional as Jackson would not be seen as a threat if he didn't also have power: the power to live his life in the manner he pleased, to dress and change his body as he pleased (although his change in skin color was due to vitiligo[52]) and, most of all, to influence others, in ways that Orth feels are dangerous.

Was bullying of Jackson by the media effective? Did the years of rumors and falsehoods about Jackson damage him in any substantive way? After all, he remained hugely popular with millions who did not feel unease at his otherness and did not find him threatening. But despite his enduring popularity, the negative media stories primed the public to believe the worst about him when he was accused of child molestation in 1993 and 2003. Once these allegations hit the media, virtually no objectivity could be found among journalists, and their reporting compounded Jackson's ostracism.

An entertainment industry expert has offered quantitative proof of the effect on Jackson of adverse media stories. After Jackson's death, his mother and children filed a wrongful death lawsuit against AEG Live, the company responsible

---

[52] Jackson announced that he had a skin disorder in his interview with Oprah Winfrey in 1993. Since Jackson's death, his vitiligo has been described by several people and was documented in his autopsy report.

for promoting the This Is It concerts, for which Jackson was preparing when he died. In July 2013, during the resulting trial, an expert testified that negative headlines had diminished Jackson's "likeability" ratings and, therefore, his earning potential. The expert cited damage to Jackson's ability to sell albums and acquire endorsements and sponsorships.[53]

Although Jackson was found not guilty at his 2005 trial for child molestation, that decisive finding did not put an end to rumors and assumptions of corruption. It also did not alter the perception of Jackson as an extraordinarily powerful figure. As we will see in the next chapter, conjecture about Jackson on the part of some writers became even more extreme and less connected to reality.

---

[53]   Alan Duke, "Bad news hurt Michael Jackson's earning potential, witness says," *CNN.com*, July 30, 2013.

CHAPTER FOUR

ANGELISM AND BEASTIALISM

The Resistible Demise of Michael Jackson was published in 2009, a few months after Jackson's death on June 25 of that year. The book is a collection of essays by 23 music writers, bloggers and academics, most of them British. It was edited by Mark Fisher, a music writer and philosophy professor living in London. Fisher states in his introduction that his purpose in assembling the book was to mark Jackson's death "by something other than facile 'tributes' or muck-raking biographies."

The authors of the essays in the book are Marcello Carlin, Robin Carmody, Joshua Clover, Sam Davies, Geeta Dayal (the sole woman), Tom Ewing, Mark Fisher, Dominic Fox, Jeremy Gilbert, Owen Hatherley, Charles Holland, Ken Hollings, Barney Hoskins, Reid Kane, Paul Lester, Suhail Malik, Ian Penman, Chris Roberts, Steven Shaviro, Mark Sinker, David Stubbs, Alex Williams and Evan Calder Williams.

The meaning of the book's title is never made clear, although the "resistible" seems to refer to the authors' resistance to succumbing to the "facile 'tributes' or muck-raking biographies" mentioned by Fisher in his introduction.

And resist they do. The book contains little in the way of heart-felt praise and no attempt at the research that even the most muck-raking biography would require. The essays are attempts to understand Jackson's cultural impact, but they are all highly critical of Jackson, ranging from cynicism to hateful name-calling, although some authors offer an occasional thoughtful insight. Geeta Dayal's article is the one exception to the general tone of the book; it is an emotionally neutral account of Jackson's visit to India and his influence on Bollywood music and dance.

The Resistible Demise is not a work of fact-based journalism, unlike Dave Marsh's book and the article by Maureen Orth, even if Marsh and Orth's research is often poorly applied or facts ignored or distorted. In The Resistible Demise, the authors draw primarily upon tabloid stories and internet rumors read over the years, and their own imaginations. None of the writers seem to have a firm grounding in the actual facts of Jackson's life.

The lack of factual reliability coupled with the extreme negativity in The Resistible Demise may appear to render it a fairly useless book. However, it can also be seen as a Rorschach test of attitudes toward Jackson, a free association that produces unconscious views along with the conscious. Therein lies its value as a work to be analyzed.

The authors' conscious positions toward Jackson are ones of skepticism, cynicism, resentment, anger and even hatred. However, what emerges, even in the teeth of this extreme negativity, is a portrayal of Jackson as having power, but power that is far beyond the sort attributed to him by Marsh and Orth, although there are some similarities. Whereas Marsh initially saw Jackson as a messianic figure who could unite all opposites in society, the writers of The Resistible Demise portray him repeatedly as divine, semi-divine and otherworldly. Orth perceived Jackson to be an elite person who manipulated and intimidated others; the authors of The

Resistible Demise describe him in terms of a powerful ruler, either benign or despotic.

The writers' complaints against Jackson fall into one or more of the following categories in every essay (with the exception of Dayal's). They complain that he was hubristic, a freak, physically corrupt and/or morally corrupt. An examination of the terminology used to describe Jackson gives the flavor of their criticism and also will demonstrate the structure of the writers' reaction to him.

The words used in the book to describe Jackson's supposed hubris are:

- monumental hubris
- vaulting ambition and Cecil De Mille-ain pretension
- megalomania (multiple times)
- messianic pomposity
- the ludicrous, breath-taking, sovereign scale of Jackson's drive
- mock-dictatorial hubris
- Lear
- narcissistic in the extreme

Nine of the authors cite as evidence of hubris Jackson's "Earth Song," the song itself as well as the accompanying short film and Jackson's live performances of it, especially at the 1996 BRIT Awards in London. Only one of those authors believes in its sincerity and praises it. The others see it as insincere and self-aggrandizing, calling it bombastic, "lachrymose," and "hubristic messianism." The BRIT Awards performance is significant to the authors because during it Jarvis Cocker, of the British band Pulp, spontaneously ran out on stage and mimed farting to signal his opinion that Jackson was presenting himself as a Christ-like figure. Cocker was quickly hustled off stage by security, and Jackson's performance was not interrupted. Although this was a very minor incident in

Jackson's career, it looms large in the minds of the writers of *The Resistible Demise*, presumably because Cocker validated their view that Jackson was overreaching and grandiose.

The authors also see hubris in Jackson's wearing of military costumes and the martial nature of his promotional campaign for his *HIStory* album. Jackson's penchant for military themes, which is misinterpreted by these authors, will be explored in Chapter Five.

The writers of *The Resistible Demise* overwhelmingly see Jackson as a freak or other, and their terms used to describe him as such are extreme:

- strange
- ambisexual
- cross-cultural role model, strange and new and difficult to read
- freakish
- inhuman
- symptom
- bizarre and indefensible
- androgynous white alien future-creature
- out-there and outrageous
- clownishly peculiar Jacko
- wounded soul in the guise of a superfreak
- elongated superfreak, a balletic stick insect
- puppet
- precious, weirdo girl-man
- wacko
- mangled Tinkerbell
- simulacrum
- quirky, shy, spaced
- drag queen puppet droog
- media clown-soul
- St. Wacko
- ambiguous

- figure of prehistoric, primordial disturbance
- ambiguity
- grotesque
- alienation from masculine norms
- ultimately incapable of intervening in the mediated spectacle of masculine posturing
- hermaphroditic James Brown
- figure of undecidability
- auto-castrated asexual
- empty core
- a kind of hideous hybrid creature
- incompossible chimera
- bony fright-wigged Wizard of Oz
- neutered
- creepy
- a never-man
- disavowed sex, disappeared sexuality
- emotionally retarded, "childlike" boy in a man's world

Related to the view of Jackson as a freak or other is the authors' perception of him as in some way physically corrupt, particularly as decaying, being held together by machinery, and/or being dead while still alive:

- like an aging millionairess
- dead while still alive
- repellant whitened sepulcher
- a biotic component going mad
- cyborg
- piece of wood
- ravaged, ruined, in immense pain
- exotically disfigured
- posthuman
- enhanced human

- grotesque parody of whiteness, a zombified, living-dead simulation of whiteness
- hideous
- skin rot
- mountainous blemishes
- physical disintegration
- disastrous architect of his own physiognomy
- silent rot beneath the skin
- decrepit
- zombie (multiple times)
- zombie Jacko
- poor wizened little fellow
- bruised
- physical collapse
- zombified, living-dead simulation of whiteness
- Afrofuturist nightmare
- a collection of discrete animated objects
- gradual decay
- not unlike Darth Vader – a degenerating husk of pale flesh kept barely alive by a complex mediating machinery
- more machine than man
- rotting interior
- disintegrating facial tissue
- unmistakable signs of necrosis were written all over his face
- amputated his own face
- Zombie Jackson
- body dysmorphic disorder
- machine
- emaciated and lily white
- living after-life
- white woman pork face
- dying king
- withered and atrophied

- death-in-life long before his own mortal death
- already dead
- living-dead
- no longer looked human
- abyss of fathomless pain
- erased and enervated and shoddily reconstructed face flesh
- scarred flesh, scared flesh
- cauterized, castrated, cut up
- hurting and fading
- zombie/Christ
- face becomes a form of mask
- white scare face
- white lady
- slave master's wife
- animatronic, robot, dummy
- lifedeath
- undead
- neither alive nor dead, neither living nor not-living
- tinsel horror

Equally extreme are the writers' terminology for Jackson's supposed moral corruption or mental illness:

- Gothic Oedipus
- a biotic component going mad
- damaged, even deranged figure of no fixed sex
- fame addled
- mad
- deeply troubled
- a mess
- a disgrace
- delirious and demented
- wreckage of a legend
- common pedophile

- never quite human
- both more than and less than human
- monster
- creature of absolute soullessness
- cyber-nought
- corporate plasticity
- a man in the grip of pantophobic neurosis
- allergic to life and disconnected from the human spirit
- crumbling mind
- noxiousness
- hidden corruption
- psychosis
- deranged
- nightmare that the dream of pop curdled intolunatic horrorshow monster
- perverted Gothic malefactor
- dehumanization
- crushed and frightened
- desperate
- beautiful and broken
- sinister, libidinal, predatory
- became a kind of psychosis or pathology
- architect of his own weirdness
- hyper-commodified celebrity
- perennially compromised public persona
- paranoid
- genuine beast of the apocalypse
- abomination
- trash (multiple times)
- hollow
- washed-up drugged up blocked entertainer
- Disney Allen Poe, Pedophile Bambi, Lovecraftian Dumbo
- a maybe/maybe-not pedophile

- a man toppled over into serious pathology
- king of painkillers
- bald, a pin cushion, narcotized beyond addiction, rich but emaciated, popular but alone, loved but adrift and untouched . . . spiritless
- isolated figure who buys further isolation to hide inside
- Vegas life of mirage and morphine
- posthumous post–human
- portentous, pissed off, poisonous
- scary
- ossifies into a kind of demented self–pity
- haunted
- terminal addict
- pedophile
- a malignant singularity, polarity, negative
- a black hole
- snake
- ghost
- King of Pain

Given this long list of terminology of moral corruption, one might conclude that the writers believe that Jackson was a pedophile, but only two of the book's authors, David Stubbs and Ian Penman, suggest or state that they believed the child sex abuse allegations against Jackson.

In the previous chapter the question was posed of whether false or exaggerated stories had been effective in damaging to Jackson, and we saw that an expert had testified that those stories had hurt his album sales and his ability to make money by endorsing products and acquiring sponsorships. A reading of all of the foregoing lists of words and phrases is further evidence that falsehoods did indeed damage his reputation. Since the writers of *The Resistible Demise* seem to primarily base their responses to Jackson on tabloid and internet rumors, rather than research, they are reflecting, and apparently believing, the bullying by the media that Jackson endured for decades. Not only do the negative terms used by the authors paint a picture of someone who is disreputable, but also of someone who seems not to even be a human being.

Despite the horrific portrait painted by the authors of *The Resistible Demise*, there is simultaneously something else of a completely different nature going on in their writing. In the midst of such extreme criticism, the authors frequently use words and phrases that describe Jackson's talents in glowing, sometimes ecstatic terms, that depict Jackson as having the a power of a king or sometimes a despot and, most surprising and most frequently, that represent him as a divine or supernatural figure. Some of these terms are used ironically or even sarcastically, but they are used nonetheless, acknowledging that this other view of Jackson is a reality that must be included, even by these critics.

As would be expected by anyone who appreciates Jackson's artistry, the writers describe his talents in extremely positive terms, although some shade into the negative by depicting his abilities as frightening:

- genius (multiple times)
- the most popular entertainer on Earth
- zeitgeist-altering starpower
- the biggest star on earth
- magnetic
- dazzling
- phenomenal
- high wattage
- a shining crossover star who would dwarf even Elvis Presley
- the biggest star on the planet
- a vision of ease, grace and energy

- technically impeccable performance which makes the blood run a little cold
- frightening talent
- possessed by dancing
- staggeringly-gifted child
- a creature of youth and lightness whose performance defies emotional gravity
- surpassingly joyful *rightness*
- megastar
- astonishing talent
- megastar
- a body commandeered by the abstract vectors and current of pure rhythm
- music as electrifying, colonizing current
- disco's most brilliant voice
- an incomparable artistic talent
- *wunderkind*
- star

The authors of *The Resistible Demise* use words and phrases, as do Dave Marsh and Maureen Orth, that show their perception of Jackson as having power. Some of them represent him as having power of a royal nature:

- king (multiple times)
- King of Pop (multiple times)
- a boy who would be king (referring to Jackson as a child)
- the new King
- Maharaja of Pop
- the True King of Rock, Pop and Soul
- the fallen King
- royal
- true royalty
- the true boy king

- king of media manipulation
- dying king
- canny ruler
- a modern prince
- King of Washington [when he visited the Reagans in the White House]

The book's essay "After pop" by Tom Ewing best expresses the view of Jackson as a king:

> A King of Pop implies a kingdom. Michael Jackson won his in the style of a medieval ruler, carving out a realm piece by piece across a hard year of campaigning. Some of his subjects bent the knee when he performed "Billie Jean" as part of a Motown anniversary special; others when he formed common cause with Eddie Van Halen or Paul McCartney. His fiefdom extended across every school playground with the release of the "Thriller" video and its body-popping zombies.[54]

However, some of the writers also see Jackson as a despot:

- totalitarian pop dictator
- despot
- Despot of Pop
- Stalin of Pop
- dictator
- fallen despot
- pantomime military dictator
- an indefatigable and pitiless pop-Reich
- rampaged across the planet
- hegemony
- Emperor Tiberius on Capri

---

[54]   *The Resistible Demise of Michael Jackson* (2009), p. 219.

The article by Owen Hatherley, entitled "'Stalin's tomb won't let me be': Michael Jackson as despot," elaborates at the greatest length on this view of Jackson. He compares Jackson to Muammar Ghadaffi, Stalin, Carlos the Jackal, Andreas Baader, Tito, Idi Amin, Jean-Bedel Bokassa and Kim Jong-Il, and mentions Hitler in passing.[55]

Truly extraordinary, however, are the words these cynical writers use to describe Jackson as a divine, semi-divine or supernatural figure:

- god (multiple times)
- Christ
- disco as theology, divine disco
- an amazing character operating at the limits of what is normally expected of a human being
- uncanny
- fey
- feyest pop star on the planet
- demi-god
- myth
- otherworldly
- larger – madder – than life
- an angel who fell to Earth
- cast a luminous ethereal aura over popular music
- supernova
- almost godlike
- utopia
- special
- wearing socks made of angel
- godhood
- holiness
- made claims toward God
- incandescent

---

[55]   Ibid., pp. 194-200.

- mercurial
- ubiquitous and withdrawn at the same time
- Second Coming
- transfiguration
- beyond the human pale
- superstar
- [Jackson's dancing] was the new world
- his dancing was out of time
- architect of his own destiny
- Michael of Everywhere-Nowhere
- a deity, a divine or semi-divine being
- an otherworldly figure of some gentility
- never appeared to be a creature of appetite
- a creature of youth and lightness whose performance defies emotional gravity
- surpassingly joyful *rightness*
- evanescent
- quasi-deity
- messianic
- apparently ageless
- apparently immortal
- gravity-defying
- outside history, outside any categories of race, gender or class
- the individual liberated from all bonds of community and history
- transcend identity and origin
- raceless and all races
- supernova
- elfin
- world-striding vastness of Jackson's extended Passion Play
- Peter Pan in Neverland
- unearthly
- invading savior

- messianic
- Gothic
- uncanny (multiple references)
- sublime
- a thing possessed
- dreaming of being human
- faun-like, fragile, elusive, victimized
- Motown's young messiah
- immortal and unmournable
- Messiah
- a true immortal
- the great god Pan
- transducer of dreams and colonizing our unconscious: like a riff, a headline, a drug, a ghost
- defied nature
- a singularity without lineage, without predecessors
- transcended the usual human script
- messiah, re-incarnation, King of Pop, imagist revolutionary
- platinum sainthood
- sainthood
- archangel
- beyond human law
- beyond the bonds of everyday anything
- specter
- pure air element: no earth, no fire
- essence, myth, imago
- avant-garde paradigm, remarkable post-Human, a kind of postmodern Gnostic liberated from mere flesh, destiny, fixed roles of race and sex
- ghost
- Christ
- electric-flash
- prophecy and resurrection
- monumental, without precedent

- trying to pretend he is without ancestors
- as if he could RE-encrypt the corrupted dyads of male -+-female, mother-+-father, black-and-white, us-and-them
- everyone's dream object, everyone's escape
- the boy without others
- uncanny
- not matter
- de-railing of coding and decoding
- postmodern dream of becoming something new

The number of these terms indicating a supernatural power and the degree of their hyperbole rival that of the terms used in the book to describe Jackson as a freak or as physically or morally corrupt. How could it be that a book that is so harshly critical of Jackson, that repeatedly represents him as barely recognizably human, would also contain an almost equal number of terms that depict him as divine or nearly so?

Even though the tone of the book is overwhelmingly antagonistic to Jackson, there is clearly a balancing between extremely positive and negative terminology going on. This is best illustrated by the book's article by Ian Penman.[56] The overall tenor of the article is extremely hostile to Jackson and it is clear that Penman was not a fan of his music. At 43 pages, this is the book's longest article and its angriest. One comes away with the impression of having witnessed Penman gleefully and repeatedly kick Jackson's lifeless body.

Penman begins by saying that it seemed that the only choice he had in writing about Jackson was between "hagiography and character assassination," implying that he intends to take a different approach. And then he proceeds to indulge in character assassination. The article is a grab bag

---

[56]   Ibid., pp. 267–309.

of disjointed rants about Jackson and, as a result, is difficult to summarize. However, Penman's main themes are that Jackson was other (specifically, unreadable in terms of gender, sexuality and race), that he was supposedly living dead or a zombie, that he was too angry, and that he was from the proletariat. Penman repeats several wild tabloid stories about Jackson as if they must be true and cites Wikipedia with the same lack of skepticism. He clearly believes the pedophilia allegations against Jackson. Penman's article rendered the largest number of negative terms and phrases describing him.

However, Penman also uses the greatest number of words that describe Jackson as having earthly or supernatural power, although Penman often uses these expressions resentfully. He calls him "a modern prince," a "postmodernist archangel," says that Jackson is among those who "transcended the usual human script," that he "slipped beyond the bonds of everyday anything," was "a singularity without lineage, without predecessors," "pure air element: no earth, no fire," an "essence, myth, imago," and "Christ."

Why is this balancing of terms occurring in *The Resistible Demise*? Another of the authors, Dominic Fox, briefly mentions the concept of angelism, an idea that is key to understanding what is going on in the book. Angelism is an unconscious theme that runs throughout *The Resistible Demise* and illuminates the apparently inexplicable balancing of extremely positive and extremely negative terminology. Angelism, which does not refer specifically to angels, is the mistaken perception that humans (or, in this case, one human) are primarily of a divine nature, to the exclusion of earthly and bodily concerns such as greed or sex. The term was coined in the 1940s by French Catholic philosopher Jacques Maritain in criticizing the ideas of René Descartes.[57]

---

[57] Richard Fafara, "Angelism and Culture," from *Understanding Maritain: Philosopher and Friend* (1987).

Angelism, however, is only one end of the polarity seen in *The Resistible Demise*. Just as in Carl Jung's idea of the "shadow" emerging to resolve the tension of opposites, the compensating element to angelism is beastialism. Beastialism, a term also coined by Maritain, is the erroneous view that humans are motivated only by greed, sex and other bodily, selfish concerns. Freud's theories, for example, can be seen as beastial, because he saw humans as being driven solely by sex, (penis) envy and violence.

The authors of *The Resistible Demise*, despite their cynicism or outright hostility toward Jackson, cannot seem to prevent themselves from acknowledging an angelistic view of him: as a figure who seemed to be beyond the bounds of mortal humans, a messiah, a saint, or even divine. We saw an early stage of this perception in Dave Marsh's book, but by the time of Jackson's death, despite years of damaging tabloid stories and allegations of child molestation, that angelistic perception seems to have grown tremendously.

Jackson's fans viewed him as angelistic because of his talents as a singer, songwriter and dancer, his many songs promoting world peace and understanding, his soft-spoken persona, his reputation for not indulging in hard partying and sex with groupies, and the fluidity of his racial and sexual identity. (We will further examine the origins of this angelistic view of Jackson in the next chapter.) While the writers of *The Resistible Demise* are not ardent fans, if fans at all, they seem to have picked up the angelistic interpretation of Jackson from his admirers and the *zeitgeist*.

By contrast, Prince and Madonna, Jackson's closest peers in the 1980s and 1990s, most frequently presented themselves in music videos, films and performances as highly sexual, that is, beastial, beings. (A notable exception is Madonna's beautiful, highly angelistic video for "Frozen" in which, wearing a long black dress, she floats above a desert and becomes a flock of black birds and then a black dog.) While

Prince and Madonna endeavored to push limits, they pushed the limits of the boxes they already inhabited, namely that of heterosexuality. Jackson simply didn't inhabit any box that anyone could identify and did not present himself primarily in terms of sexuality. In the next chapter we will examine the ways that Jackson's music videos contributed to an angelistic image.

The seed of the negative backlash toward Jackson may have been in the need felt by some to compensate for an unrealistically angelistic view of Jackson with an equally unrealistic beastial view. As Owen Hatherley states in the first sentence of his article, "the opposite of Neverland [Jackson's beautiful home that included an amusement park and zoo] is Gary, Indiana [the grungy industrial city of Jackson's birth]."

The writers of *The Resistible Demise* do not trust the view of Jackson as an angelistic being. And, of course, they are correct not to trust it. Despite the unearthly quality of his talent and presentation of his public persona, Jackson was a human being with as many flaws as the rest of us. But the writers of *The Resistible Demise* do not bother to consider or investigate this possibility. Instead, they react to their distrust by looking for and inventing a beastiality for Jackson that is too extreme to be even remotely realistic, as is the angelistic side. Put another way by Walker Percy, whose novel *Love in the Ruins* revolves around the poles of angelism and beastialism, "So to treat angelism, you walk through a swamp."[58]

In his essay,[59] Dominic Fox states that ". . otherworldly talent requires compensation in the form of lurid displays of all-too-human weakness," and "defy nature and your face will fall off!" Fox seems to be saying that Jackson's otherworldly talent (angelism) required him to compensate with "displays

---

[58] Walker Percy, *Love in the Ruins* (1971), p. 36.
[59] *The Resistible Demise of Michael Jackson*, pp. 89-95.

of all-too-human weakness" and physical decay (beastialism), but he misunderstands the locus of the angelism and the beastialism. The locus is in the perception of Jackson, not within Jackson himself. There is no evidence that Jackson thought of himself as divine or supernatural; that perception was the province of his audience. Of course Jackson had human faults and weaknesses, but the most extreme views of him, that his face and body were falling apart, that he was a pedophile, that he consumed enormous amounts of drugs at every opportunity, and that he was mentally ill are not supported by a thoughtful examination of his life.

Most of the essays in *The Resistible Demise* reflect these extreme opposites. Steven Shiviro begins with angelistic descriptions of Jackson: "He was a vision of ease, grace and energy. . . Michael Jackson was a supernova; we loved him, we worshipped him, we found his appearances and performances almost godlike." By the end of his piece Shaviro depicts Jackson in a beastial light: "posthuman," "a kind of grotesque parody of whiteness, a zombified, living-dead simulation of whiteness," and "delirious and demented."[60]

Jeremy Gilbert calls Jackson's dancing "miraculous," his music "hymns to becoming," and describes him as "the apparently ageless, apparently immortal, gravity-defying, graceful Michael Jackson," but concludes that Jackson ended up as "decrepit, deranged and broke."[61]

Mark Sinker writes about "the unearthly body of his voice" and his attempt to "unite and heal . . . all the shattered, crashing forces of the world," but ends with descriptions of Jackson as "zombie Jacko" and a "poor wizened little fellow."[62]

Describing Jackson as a conquering king who had "an astonishing talent," Tom Ewing quotes Rob Harvilla of the

---

[60] Ibid., pp. 51–62.
[61] Ibid., pp. 137–149.
[62] Ibid. pp. 164–187.

Village Voice, who tweeted the day after Jackson died, "Dude had unimaginable power." But Ewing goes on to write, "the King Jackson most resembles is Lear, maddened and howling at the storm."[63]

Although David Stubbs begins by calling Jackson "mercurial, phenomenal, high-wattage" and says that "his appearances had the intoxicating, rarefied air of a Second Coming," he concludes that "[h]e was a freak . . . a man who became practically allergic to life and disconnected from the human spirit" and "a man in the grip of a pantophobic neurosis."[64]

Sam Davies says that "his talent, for singing, dancing, performing, was sublime" and "Michael Jackson was the world's first megastar . . . able to fuse the visual and musical in a way that neither The Beatles nor Elvis could, saturating the world with a spectacular image of himself and setting a pop paradigm in which the new, totalized star must sing, dance, act, endorse products and franchise themselves at once." But Davies then expounds the theory that Jackson was "the world's first Gothic megastar," defining Gothic as "a state of uncertainty in which one is not sure if an apparently living object is really alive or if an apparently inanimate object is alive."[65]

Writing that "Michael was Motown's young messiah, disco's most brilliant voice, an incomparable artistic talent cutting through dance music, R&B, soul, and driving them all toward something greater," Reid Kane then concludes that after Jackson recorded *Off the Wall* he "became not unlike Darth Vader – a degenerating husk of pale flesh kept barely alive by a complex mediating machinery."[66]

---

[63] Ibid., pp. 219–225.
[64] Ibid., pp. 69–80.
[65] Ibid., pp. 226–232.
[66] Ibid., pp. 233–242.

Ian Penman, the most intensely polarized of the books authors, writes, "I've read postmodern theory that posits Michael as kind of avant-garde paradigm, remarkable post-Human, a kind of postmodern Gnostic liberated from mere flesh, destiny, fixed roles of race and sex." Just a few sentences later, he presents an equally exaggerated, beastial interpretation of Jackson, a "walk through the swamp":

> Because after a certain point, being Michael Jackson seemed to involve an abyss of fathomless pain. The irony being that his life had become all too fatally a thing of FLESH. Erased and enervated and shoddily reconstructed face flesh. Child's flesh. Crimes of the flesh, scarred flesh, scared flesh. Cauterized, castrated, cut up . . . Pain. Legs. Head. Nose. Hip. Demerol. Morphine. Dilaudid. Sex. Masturbation. Public hair made public. Circumcision. Test tube. Bald.[67]

Penman puts it more succinctly when he says, "What heaven, what hell."

The same principal of opposites is also clearly evident in the essay "True enough: Michael in fifty shards" by Chris Roberts.[68] This article is comprised of fifty brief imaginary vignettes of Jackson's life, from birth to death, the tone of which ranges from disrespectful and sarcastic to hateful. It is rife with beastial images of Jackson: Jackson's nose travels by itself around the world; Jackson is jealous when Elizabeth Taylor gets married again; his chimpanzee Bubbles defecates all over his mansion, which begins to smell; he reads from the Book of Job, "My skin is black upon me and my bones are burned with heat"; he thinks about aging; he looks in the

---

[67]   Ibid., p. 275.
[68]   Ibid., pp. 96-136.

mirror and is reminded of Dali's melting clocks; he swallows huge handfuls of pills.

But Roberts interweaves images of a clearly angelistic nature: "Michael is born. A skylark flies overhead"; Jackson starts to work on an elixir of youth, using honey, emeralds, stardust and the tears of small babies; for the making of *Thriller* Jackson orders mountains, lakes, clouds, planets, moons and comets; he has several conversations with an okapi and one with a caterpillar; he makes plans to go to the moon; when Jackson dies a skylark drinks his elixir of youth and lives forever.

Just as the angelistic view of Jackson is too extreme to be real, the beastial view is equally improbable. Just as common sense tells us that he could not have been a "messiah," "demi-god," "beyond the human pale," "not matter," or "an angel who fell to earth," and he was equally unlikely to have been a "zombie," a "lunatic horrorshow monster," a "genuine beast of the apocalypse," "delirious and demented," or a "totalitarian pop dictator." Large numbers of people came to fully believe one extreme or the other, however.

Both the angelism and the beastialism arise from Jackson's otherness and his unreadability. Unreadability affords opportunity for projection, and the angelism and beastialism are both projections of great hope and great fear: the hope that a man could have the power to rise above earthly constraints and concerns, and the fear that such a person is evil and subject to grotesque physical decay.

Let us now look more closely at the origins of the view of Jackson as powerful and angelistic.

CHAPTER FIVE

ORIGINS OF POWER

We have seen that even Michael Jackson's severest critics saw him as an extraordinarily powerful figure, in ways that far exceeded the usual attributes of fame and wealth. He was seen as elite or royalty or as a ruler or as having supernatural qualities, and his power was in large part derived from the very characteristics that made some uncomfortable, his otherness.

Dave Marsh saw Jackson originally as a figure with the power to transform society into being more accepting of differences, or at least as someone who could inspire that dream in others. Maureen Orth saw Jackson as sinister figure who had the power to manipulate others through his refusal to abide by society's rules. The authors of *The Resistible Demise of Michael Jackson* perceived Jackson to be powerful in the sense of royalty or a ruler or as a supernatural being, although many of those authors were resentful of his power.

Of course, if his critics perceived Jackson as powerful and even supernatural, his fans were even more susceptible to that view. The angelistic view of Jackson was more extreme among his fans, and some even saw him as a literal angel. Dozens of images of Jackson as an angel can be found on the internet, and a couple of books have been published that proclaim him as an angel. Photographer David LaChapelle has created an ironic "American Jesus" series, modeled on Mexican saint cards, consisting of three images of Jackson as a religious icon, including that of the Archangel Michael (Jackson) subduing Satan. In September 2009, shortly after Jackson's death, a barely ironic chapel-like art installation entitled "The Cult of Michael Jackson" by artist Rusel Parish opened in Brooklyn. How did this astonishing view of Jackson as a powerful, supernatural being come about? Did Jackson deliberately seek to be seen this way?

Perceptions of Jackson as a person with unusual power began even before his adult solo career got under way. James Situp, who was band director and pianist for The Jacksons, noticed a change in Jackson in 1977, when he was 19 years old:

> Everyone who dealt with him closely, family included, began to tread softly when dealing with Michael. The quiet power he was gaining was amazing to me. I'd never seen anyone have that much influence over people without having a stern attitude. I noticed that when he spoke, people were starting to listen. He was still outvoted on things [by his family], but now it was a bit more reluctantly. Joseph and the brothers were beginning to give him space. I began to notice that if they saw one iota of displeasure in his face, they began to get worried. For sure, things were changing as Michael was growing up.[69]

Photographer Todd Gray, who worked with Jackson for over ten years, recalls first speaking to him in December 1979

---

[69]   J. Randy Taraborrelli, *Michael Jackson: The Magic, The Madness, The Whole Story* (2009), p. 164.

in a dressing room crowded with family, friends and record company executives:

> Almost everyone in the room was trying to get Michael's attention. Everyone. Each new person who entered greeted Jackie, Marlon, Randy, and Tito, but soon let them alone. It was clear that Michael was the one who had the juice in the room, and everybody was jockeying for position to get his attention, to catch his eye."[70]

Despite the power that some who knew Jackson saw, he still had to struggle to gain acceptance by the public and critics, even at the height of his fame. One of the ways he attempted to do this was through wearing military-style clothing. Some of the authors of *The Resistible Demise* complained resentfully that Jackson seemed to be a dictator or despot, citing as evidence Jackson's wearing of military uniforms and his martial-tinged promo films. On the surface, this proclivity for the military seems puzzling since nothing about Jackson's music or personality seemed authoritarian, the one exception being that he "militarized" live performances of "They Don't Care About Us" by performing it with dancers dressed as soldiers. An examination of Jackson's history shows why he would have been drawn to military clothing and themes and the purposes they served.

Jackson felt deeply wounded by being snubbed at the Grammy Awards after the release of *Off the Wall*, as noted in Chapter Two. During the *Off the Wall* period, Jackson had performed in tuxedos or soft, spangly jumpsuits and made public appearances in street clothes, but with the release of *Thriller* he began appearing often in military uniforms.

The reason for this change in clothing preference is suggested by Michael Bush, who was the co-designer and

---

[70]   Todd Gray, *Michael Jackson: Before He Was King* (2009), p. 13.

co-creator of Jackson's stage costumes and other apparel from 1984 until the end of his life. Bush and his partner Dennis Tompkins were asked by Jackson to create military costumes and clothes that were cut along military lines. Bush says that Jackson loved these sorts of clothes because they fit well, lent him an air of authority and "commanded attention and respect."[71] No doubt Jackson began wearing military clothing after *Thriller* was released because of the statement they made about how he wanted to be perceived and treated, not as a ruler, and certainly not as a despot, but with the respect he felt he deserved.

During the *Thriller* period the media began to criticize Jackson in a very personal way, not always with a firm basis in fact, and Jackson's intelligence and agency as an artist were often questioned, as we saw with Dave Marsh's book. Clearly, no one could ignore Jackson after *Thriller*, but as the criticism continued and the tabloid stories about him grew wilder, he continued to fight for artistic legitimacy. In 1988, *Rolling Stone* readers voted Jackson "Worst Male Singer," "Most Unwelcome Comeback" and "Worst Dressed Male Singer," and the *Bad* album's tour as second "Worst Tour of the Year." With that kind of pubic backlash, it is not surprising that he would have felt the need to continue for many years to present himself in clothing specifically designed to engender respect. Jackson continued to perform and make appearances in military uniforms through late 1997, when the tour for his *HIStory* album ended.

The military theme also appeared in the short promo films for his albums *Dangerous* and *HIStory*, where Jackson is shown in military costume running or marching with police or soldiers. This is not the overwhelming theme of the *Dangerous* promo, but the militarization reaches surreal, giddy

---

71   Bush, Michael, *The King of Style: Dressing Michael Jackson* (2012), p. 9.

heights in the promo for *HIStory*. The film features Jackson, in a black and silver military uniform, walking and smiling at the head of thousands of computer-generated soldiers, with a triumphal arch and winged victory figures atop tall columns in the background. A statue of Jackson that appears to be at least twenty stories tall is unveiled to fireworks, screaming crowds and fainting women. Jackson's promotional campaign for the *HIStory* album also included placing several very large statues of himself in London and other European cities. It is likely that this promo film and the statues, more than anything else Jackson did, gave rise to the accusations in *The Resistible Demise* that he was a dictator or despot.

The *HIStory* promo seems to be completely inconsistent with Jackson's soft-spoken persona and the nature of his music. It is only possible to explain this over-the-top film and the apparently self-aggrandizing statues by considering the context of Jackson's life at the time. The promo was filmed in Prague in August 1994, only seven months after he had settled the civil suit against him for child sexual abuse. Jackson always maintained that he had never abused any child, and those who knew him said that he was distraught by the 1993 charges. The majority of the songs on the *HIStory* album seem to have been written in response to that difficult experience. If a military theme was one of Jackson's ways of sending the message that he was worthy of respect, it makes a great deal of sense that he would have ratcheted up that theme following the 1993 allegations. He may have over-shot the mark, however, leading to a backlash in some critics.

But many saw Jackson in a ruler mode without being prompted by Jackson himself. Although he has often been criticized for "crowning himself" as the King of Pop in 1991 by asking MTV to refer to him regularly by that title,[72]

---

[72] Michael Goldberg, "The Making of 'The King of Pop,'" *Rolling Stone*, January 9, 1992.

perceptions of him as royalty began years earlier. In 1983, *Rolling Stone* writer Gerri Hirshey called him "a young prince of pop."[73] In reviewing one of the Victory tour concerts in 1984, Nelson George described Jackson as a supernaturally tinged royal figure: "a fairy prince off in the distance, far removed and detached from his subjects." George did not find that particular performance satisfactory, but he was extremely impressed by a later performance in the tour, after which he concluded that "Springsteen may be the boss and Prince the royal contender, but guess who still wears the crown."[74]

In 1985, pop music satirist Weird Al Yankovic also portrayed Jackson as a royal figure, one with supernatural powers. Yankovic's mockumentary about himself called *The Compleat Al* contains a six-minute comic depiction of how he asked Jackson if he could parody his song "Beat It." Yankovic's film shows Jackson not only as powerful, but shows Jackson's power as emanating from his otherness.

The film clip begins with Yankovic approaching a large mansion on a dark and stormy night. He knocks on the front door, using the Grammy doorknocker, and a suave, silver-haired butler, draped with a boa constrictor, opens the door. Yankovic enters fearfully. As he passes a painted portrait of a woman, the painting's eyes follow him with laser lights. Yankovic then enters an ancient chamber, and the door slams behind him. Back-lit by eerie light is a silent figure, who appears to be Jackson, sitting on a throne. The figure is wearing a glittery blue military jacket, sunglasses, one white glove, white socks and has Jheri curls. His face is never shown, and, of course, he is an actor playing Jackson. Yankovic, stammering with fear, asks Jackson if he could

[73] Gerri Hirshey, "Inside the Magical Kingdom," *Rolling Stone*, February 17, 1983.
[74] Nelson George, "Chocolate Chips at the Ice Capades," *Village Voice*, August 7, 1984.

make a parody of "Beat It," called "Eat It," and he begins to describe the lyrics. As he is talking, Jackson hand-feeds raw meat to a tiger. Then a chimpanzee, dressed in a glittery blue military jacket, drops onto Yankovic's lap, kisses him and runs away. Yankovic, gulping, asks Jackson what he thinks of his parody idea. Jackson wavers for a long 24 seconds between giving Yankovic a thumbs-up or a thumbs-down, finally settling on a thumbs-up. Yankovic jumps up, delirious with joy, and shakes Jackson's hand. As he jubilantly leaves the chamber, saying, "What a nice guy," Jackson begins to transform into a werewolf.

Of course, Yankovic's image of Jackson transforming into a werewolf is derived from the "Thriller" short film. (Jackson always called his music videos short films.) Jackson talked throughout his adult life of the value he placed upon "magic," as Dave Marsh so peevishly noted, especially in the sense of giving his audience a magical, escapist experience. Jackson often presented himself in his short films as having magical powers, especially the power to transform from one state of being to another. And, of course, a being who has magical powers and can transform at will is angelistic.

In the short film for "Thriller," Jackson transforms into a werewolf, back to himself, into a zombie, then back to himself, and back and forth between himself and a zombie a couple more times. In the final shot, he appears to be himself, but his eyes have become those of the werewolf seen at the beginning of the film. In "Billie Jean," everything Jackson touches lights up, he turns a homeless man's rags into a white tuxedo, and toward the end Jackson becomes invisible but continues to light up the sidewalk as he walks. Jackson appears out of a swirl of sand in "Remember the Time," and then exits by becoming sand again and blowing away.

"Black or White" is full of transformations and magical movement between settings. Jackson magically moves between scenes with African, Indonesian, American Indian,

Indian, and Russian dancers. His dancing with Russians
becomes the scene within a snow globe held by two babies.
He then dances through flames, a burning cross and a tank
firing, dances with children on a city stoop, and dances in the
torch of the Statue of Liberty. As the song ends, the camera
pulls back to show the film studio and, in the back, a black
panther, who growls and slinks out the back door into a
dark alley. The panther becomes Jackson, who then dances
accompanied only by the growls of the panther and his own
yelling. Although this gritty second half of the film is a stark
contrast to the fantastical first half, it then ends with Jackson
transforming into the panther again and leaving the alley.

Some of Jackson's short films have other sorts of
supernatural transformations. In "Bad" he undergoes a
dramatic, magical costume change (at which point the film
goes from black and white to color) and alters his relationship
with his criminally inclined friends through dancing and
singing. Similarly, in "Beat It" Jackson stops a gang fight
with his dancing, and in "Smooth Criminal" he changes a
dangerous crowd into a friendly one through dance.

The film for "You Are Not Alone" does not show any
transformations, but is notable because its literal angelism.
The version that appears only on the DVD collection *HIStory
on Film, Volume II* opens with Jackson as an angel, wearing
large wings and standing in a pool of water with a waterfall
behind him. This image recurs throughout the film and ends
the film. The image of Jackson as an angel was edited out for
later DVD collections of his short films.

Transformations run throughout the 38-minute extended
version of "Ghosts," a short film made in 1996, which was
written by Jackson and Stephen King. The film is rife with
themes of otherness, power, the public's response to Jackson
and his response to his critics. The opening scene is a dark
and stormy night in Normal Valley. A sign says "Welcome
to Normal Valley . . . nice regular people." Citizens carrying

torches, led by a portly, white middle-aged mayor, played by Jackson, approach the gate of an old mansion. A plaque on the mansion's gate reads, "Someplace Else." As they approach, a child says, "Why don't we just leave him alone? He hasn't hurt anybody. Can't we just go?" The mayor (Jackson) says angrily, "He's a weirdo. There's no place in this town for weirdos." The gate opens, and the crowd approaches the house. The front door of the mansion opens to reveal an old but magnificent house, full of cobwebs. The people enter fearfully and the front door closes. Double doors then open onto a ballroom, the crowd enters, and the film changes from black and white to color. A figure draped in black with a skull for a face appears, and the people are terrified. (The skull has no nose, just 2 holes, echoing the rumor that Jackson's nose was so disfigured by plastic surgery that it could not support a tip.) The figure lowers its skull mask a bit, revealing Jackson's eyes. The children smile and relax.

(Note the parallels with Al Yankovic's film, in which a fearful person approaches a dark mansion on a stormy night, enters the mansion with great apprehension, and then encounters Jackson in a large chamber.)

The mayor says to Jackson, "You're weird, you're strange, and I don't like you. You're scaring these kids." Jackson replies that scaring people is just for fun, and the mayor threatens to "get rough, if we have to," acknowledging the potentially serious consequences of being seen as a freak, weirdo or other.

Jackson says to the mayor, "You're trying to scare me, aren't you?" He challenges the mayor to a game in which the first one to get scared has to leave. They then engage in verbal sparring, Jackson calls forth a large group of ghosts, who alternately frighten, awe and delight the citizens but infuriate the mayor, and Jackson dances with the ghosts. He undergoes several transformations throughout the film: he peels off his face leaving just a skull, he becomes a skeleton, and he becomes a character called Superghoul, who eventually scares the mayor so badly that he exits the ballroom through a closed window, leaving Jackson the winner of their game.

The mayor also is transformed during the film. Towards the end, the mayor's face becomes a grotesque, ugly version of himself. Looking in a mirror, he says to himself, "Who's scary now? Who's the freak now? Freaky-boy, freak, circus freak! Who's scary? Who's weird now?" Jackson seems to be asking his critics to look at themselves honestly, to recognize the otherness that all of us have in some measure and to understand that we all are vulnerable to bullying.

One of the most important attributes contributing to the perception of Jackson as supernatural, and which emanated from Jackson himself rather than from special effects in a film, was his dancing. The fluidity of transformations seen in the short films becomes a more literal fluidity in his extraordinary dancing. Significantly, throughout *Ghosts*, Jackson exerts supernatural power over his troupe of ghosts through movement alone. He brings them forth and controls their actions through hand gesture, foot stamping and finger snapping, rather than through speaking or singing. And the main action of the film takes place in a ballroom, a space designed for dancing, as if to say that he knows that is a place where he reigns and has power and where his otherness works for him.

But the short films are obviously performances, not representations of Jackson as a real person. The authors examined in this book did not seem to see his power, even supposed supernatural power, solely as an illusion of Jackson's art.; they seemed to see Jackson the human being as possessing that extraordinary power. Did Jackson intend for others to see him himself as a powerful, angelistic being? The answer to this question is a qualified yes.

In 1979, when Jackson was 21 years old, he wrote down his vision for his career, a document that his team came to call his "manifesto." The manifesto reads in part:

> MJ will be my new name. No more Michael
> Jackson. I want a whole new character, a whole
> new look. I should be a tottally different person.
> People should never think of me as the kid who
> sang "ABC," "I Want You Back." I should be
> a new, incredible actor/singer/dancer that will
> shock the world. I will do no interviews. I will
> be magic. I will be a perfectionist, a researcher, a
> trainer, a masterer.[75] [sic]

Jackson clearly states in the manifesto that he intends to be someone who transforms himself into a "tottally different person" and to "be magic." The manifesto does not seem to distinguish between how he wanted to be seen as an artist and performer and how he wanted to be seen as a person.

In keeping with his manifesto, Jackson indeed transformed himself into a totally different person, a change that does almost seem to be "magic." Possibly the most startling period of Jackson's transformation is from the time that *Thriller* was released in December 1982 to the release of his *Bad* album in August 1986. In the space of a little more than three and a half years he went from appearing to be African American to having pale skin and a thinner nose, signifiers of "whiteness." His demeanor also changed significantly during this time. During the *Thriller* years he seemed to be shy, sometimes to the point of being withdrawn, and often wore mirrored sunglasses in public, as if he felt the need to hide or be protected. By the time of *Bad*, he no longer habitually wore sunglasses and showed a confidence and buoyancy not previously seen. As was his plan, by this point it was very difficult to imagine that he was the same person who had been the child lead singer for the Jackson 5. It is this sort of

---

[75] *Sixty Minutes*, CBS, May 19, 2013; and Chiderah Monde, "Michael Jackson 1979 manifesto reveals singer's plan to become the most 'incredible' entertainer," *New York Daily News*, May 20, 1979.

transformation that may have led Jeremy Gilbert, one of the authors of *The Resistible Demise*, to describe him as "outside history, outside any categories of race, gender or class."[76]

In his manifesto, Jackson declared that he would give no interviews, immediately followed by the statement that he would "be magic," implying that he felt that minimizing his public exposure would enhance his mystique. While he did sit for interviews, he did not do so often and went for long periods without giving any interviews at all. He talked to Rabbi Shumley Boteach about the mistake he felt other artists made in making frequent public appearances, the value of limiting his own public exposure and "the power of being hidden": "Halley's Comet is no more of a miracle than the moon or the sun. But we make a big deal about it because you see it once in a lifetime and everybody's out there to see it."[77] In *The Resistible Demise*, David Stubbs was responding to that strategy when he wrote, ". . . his appearances had the intoxicating, rarefied air of a Second Coming, or transfiguration."[78]

It is doubtful, however, that Jackson intended for the careful parceling out of his public appearances to make him appear to be a divine being, as Stubbs suggests. He told Rabbi Boteach that he saw that his fans sometimes reacted as if seeing him was a religious experience, but "I'm representing the higher being. I'm not saying I'm God, but I'm saying heal the planet, heal the world, save our children, save the forest."[79] His cultivation of a public image of himself as mysterious and even magic does not mean that he intended for Dave Marsh to see him as a messianic figure or for many of the authors of *The Resistible Demise* to see him as nearly divine, much less for Maureen Orth to see him as a master manipulator.

---

[76]   *The Resistible Demise of Michael Jackson*, p. 139.
[77]   Rabbi Shumley Boteach, *The Michael Jackson Tapes* (2009), p. 143.
[78]   *The Resistible Demise of Michael Jackson*, p. 70.
[79]   Boteach, *The Michael Jackson Tapes*, p. 167.

People who are perceived to have power, of any kind, are likely to encounter some who want to undermine that power. Jackson wanted to be so "incredible" that he would "shock the world," but it does not appear that he anticipated the underside of that perception: that some would come to see him as a freak or morally suspect and seek to diminish him.

Jackson's unreadability and fluidity, his otherness, as a performer and as a public persona, were tremendously inspiring and exciting to many. His otherness led some to see him as beyond normal human limitations, as supernatural, a response he clearly intended to encourage to some degree, although some of his otherness simply emanated from who he genuinely was. But he could not have anticipated the suspicion, resentment and bullying that were also responses to the angelistic perception of him.

It is remarkable, however, that after decades of hostile, inaccurate coverage by the media, the image of Jackson as a powerful, angelistic being survived. While one would expect such a view of Jackson from his fans, it is surprising to find such strong evidence of it in the writings of his critics.

The idea of Jackson as an angelistic, shape-shifter who seemed free of the bonds of ordinary human existence is very appealing to many; the idea of him as someone who tried to fool the world but was actually physically decaying and morally corrupt appeals to others in a different way. The more interesting story of Jackson is how he could conceive of the goal of appearing to be "magic," manage to give the impression of near-divinity, and the wonderful and terrible consequences of doing so. Michael Jackson was not a supernatural being or a monster; he was a fascinating, complicated person who generated an intense, complex public response. One day we may be able to move past the polarized, unrealistic views of Jackson and come to understand more about the human being.

SOURCES

Boehm, Erich, "Mirror cracks in apology in Jackson suit," *Variety*, November 10, 1998.

Boteach, Shmuley, *The Michael Jackson Tapes*, Vanguard Press, 2009.

Bush, Michael, *The King of Style: Dressing Michael Jackson*, Insight Editions, 2012

Calligan, Michael, ed., *Penal Code 1993: Abridged California Edition*, Quik-Code Publications, 1993.

Cascio, Frank, *My Friend Michael: An Ordinary Friendship with an Extraordinary Man*, William Morrow, 2011.

Chicago Tribune, "Michael Jackson Wins $2.7 Million Suit Against Writer," April 10, 1998.

Duke, Alan, "Bad news hurt Michael Jackson's earning potential, witness says," *CNN.com*, July 30, 2013.

Etherington-Smith, Meredith, *The Persistence of Memory: A Biography of Salvador Dali*, Da Capo Press, 1995.

Fafara, Richard, "Angelism and Culture," from *Understanding Maritain: Philosopher and Friend*, Deal Wyatt Hudson and Matthew J. Mancini, ed., Mercer University Press, 1987.

Fast, Susan, "The Difference That Exceeded Understanding: Remembering Michael Jackson (1959-2009)," *Popular Music and Society*, Vol. 33, No. 2, May 2010.

Fischer, Mary A, "Was Michael Jackson Framed?" *GQ*, October 1994 (also published as a book by Argo Navis Author Services in 2003).

Fisher, Mark, ed., *The Resistible Demise of Michael Jackson*, Zero Books, 2009.

Gardner, Howard, *Creating Minds*, Basic Books, 2011.

Goldberg, Michael, "The Making of 'The King of Pop,'" *Rolling Stone*, January 9, 1992.

Gordon, Cathy, "Michael Jackson settles case," *The Independent*, November 10, 1998.

Grant, Adrian, *Michael Jackson: A Visual Documentary*, Omnibus Press, 2009.

Gray, Todd, *Michael Jackson Before He Was King*, Chronicle Books, 2009.

Jackson, Michael, *Moonwalk,* Harmony Books, 2009.

Jones, Aphrodite, *Michael Jackson Conspiracy*, Aphrodite Jones Books, an iUniverse, Inc. Imprint, 2007.

Kieffer, Christine C., Ph.D., "Rumors and Gossip As Forms of Bullying: Sticks and Stones?" *Psychoanalytic Inquiry*, Vol. 33, Issue 2, March 2013, pages 90-104.

Marsh, Dave, *Trapped: Michael Jackson and the Crossover Dream*, Bantam Books, 1985.

Monde, Chiderah, "Michael Jackson 1979 manifesto reveals singer's plan to become the most 'incredible' entertainer," *New York Daily News*, May 20, 1979.

Orth, Maureen, "Losing His Grip," *Vanity Fair*, April 2003.

Orth, Maureen, "Michael Jackson is Gone, But the Sad Facts Remain," *Vanity Fair*, June 2009.

Pareles, Jon, "Michael Jackson Is Angry, Understand?", *New York Times*, June 18, 1995.

Percy, Walker, *Love in the Ruins*, Farrar, Straus & Giroux, 1971.

Risling, Greg, "Anthony Pellicano Lawsuits: Imprisoned Hollywood Private Detective's Clients Facing Hefty Bill," Associated Press, October 25, 2012.

Sixty Minutes, CBS, May 19, 2013.

Stillwater, Willa., *M Poetica*, Kindle book, 2011

Sunstein, Cass R., *On Rumors: How Falsehoods Spread, Why We Believe Them, What Can Be Done*, Farrar, Straus & Giroux, 2009.

Taraborrelli, J. Randy, *Michael Jackson: The Magic & The Madness*, Grand Central Publishing, 2009.

Vogel, Joseph, *Featuring Michael Jackson: Collected Writings on the King of Pop*, Baldwin Books, 2012.

Vogel, Joseph, *Man in the Music*, Sterling: *The Creative Life and Works of Michael Jackson*, 2011.

White, Timothy, *Catch a Fire: The Life of Bob Marley*, Henry Holt and Company, Inc., 1998.

ACKNOWLEDGMENTS

My thanks to Angus Woodward, Jalan Woodward, and Angela Woodward, relatives and all teachers of writing, for their suggestions for the manuscript. Michael Herb, I greatly appreciate your unflagging interest in hearing about my ideas and all of the beautiful drawings of Michael Jackson that you have made for me. And I thank John Branca and the Michael Jackson estate for their encouragement.

About the Author

Susan Woodward is a psychoanalytically trained clinical social worker who lives in New York City. She can be contacted at mj.othernessandpower@gmail.com.

Made in the USA
Lexington, KY
05 June 2014